The Aräqe Dilemma

The Socioeconomics of Traditional Distilled Alcohol Production, Marketing, and Consumption in Ethiopia

Yeraswork Admassie
&
Ezana Amdework

Forum for Social Studies
Addis Ababa

© 2010 by the author and Forum for Social Studies (FSS)

All rights reserved.

Printed in Addis Ababa

FSS Monograph No. 6

ISBN: 978-99944-50-36-7

Forum for Social Studies (FSS)
P.O. Box 25864 code 1000
Addis Ababa, Ethiopia
Email: fss@ethionet.et
Web: www.fssethiopia.org.et

This Monograph was published with the financial support of the Department for International Development (DFID, UK), the Embassy of Ireland, the Embassy of Denmark, and the Royal Embassy of Norway.

Contents

Acknowledgements   v

List of Illustrations   vii

List of Tables   viii

List of Boxes   ix

List of Annexes   x

I. Introduction   1
   1.1 Background   1
   1.2 Alcoholic Drinks: Origin, Classification and Nomenclature   2
   1.3 Objectives   4
   1.4 Method   5
   1.5 Scope   10

II. Brief Profile of the Study Areas   13

III. Introduction and Spread of *Aräqe*   15
   3.1 General Trends in the Amounts of *Aräqe* Produced, Marketed and Consumed   16
   3.2 New Marketing Trends: Long-Distance Trade, Roadside Peddling, and Multiple Operations   17

IV. *Äräqé* Production   19
   4.1 The Process of Production   20
   4.2 Significance of *Aräqe* Production   35
   4.3 Impacts of *Aräqe* Production   40

V. *Äräqé* Marketing   47

	5.1	Wholesale Trade	47
	5.2	Retail Trade	57
	5.3	Significance of *Aräqe* Marketing	63
	5.4	Impact of *Aräqe* Marketing	65
VI.		*Aräqé* Consumption	69
	6.1	Current Patterns and Emerging Trends in Aräqe Consumption	69
	6.2	Impacts of *Aräqe* Consumption	77
	6.3	Direct Economic Impacts	86
	6.4	Indirect and Opportunity Costs of Aräqe Consumption	88
	6.5	The Cumulative Impact of Aräqe Consumption on Society	89
VII		Local and National Measures for Regulating Alcohol	91
	7.1	Local-Level Counter-Measures	91
	7.2	Developments in the Policy and Institutional Environment for the Regulation of Alcohol	92
VIII.		Conclusions and Recommendations	99
	8.1	Synoptic Balance Sheet of the Pros and Cons	99
	8.2	The Way Forward	101
Annexes			107
References			119

Acknowledgements

This study would not have come to fruition without the kind support and facilitation of a number of institutions and individuals in the study areas. The authors gratefully acknowledge their indebtedness to the Sululta *Wäräda* Administration, Gorfo *Qäbäle* Administration, Dubär Municipal Administration, Bassona Wärana *Wäräda* Administration, Qäyït *Qäbäle* Administration, Däbrä Bïrhan Municipal Administration, *Qäbäle* 02 Administration of Däbrä Bïrhan Town, Dämbäč'a *Wäräda* Administration, Dämbäč'a *Wäräda* Municipal Administration, Yäšäboč *Qäbäle* Administration, Čäha *Wäräda* Administration, Ïmdïbïr Municipal Administration, Yäfeq-T'äräq *Qäbäle* Administration, and Arsi Nägälle Municipal Administration.

We would also like to convey our thanks to those individuals who tirelessly facilitated the collection of relevant data in their respective study areas, namely, Ato Abbu Bekele, Ato Abebayehu Belayneh, Ato Dejene Yefru, Wäizäro Abbonesh Tameru, Ato Dagnachew Andualem, Ato Geremew Nesrane, and Ato Guta Gebremariam.

Likewise, we extend our gratitude to the 124 *aräqe* distillers, retailers, and wholesalers; farmers, businessmen, elders, community and spiritual leaders as well as extension workers, teachers, health workers, police officers, and local government officials who kindly informed the study through individual and group interviews.

Our special thanks go to Ato Dawit Dikasso, Deputy Director General of the Ethiopian Food, Medicine and Health Care Administration and Control Authority, and Dr Solomon Teferra of the Department of Psychiatry, Addis Ababa University, who were kind enough to sit for an in-depth interview; Ato Zegeye Asfaw, Executive Director of *Hunde*, who provided the study with important information on the experience the NGO he heads has had in Sululta *Wäräda*, and whose advice, together with that of Dr Birhanu Adenew, was crucial to the site selection and entering the field in Sululta in a smooth manner; Ato Deresse Getachew of the Department of Sociology, AAU, who participated at the initial stage of the study and contributed towards the articulation of the objectives of the study; Dr Zemedie Asfaw, authoritative Ethiopian ethno-botanist, of the Department of Biology, AAU, who helped with finding the right scientific appellations for several local terms; Dr Johan Helland of Chr. Michelsen Institute, Norway, and Dr Araya Asfaw of the Department of Physics, AAU, whose help in identifying and accessing important materials on the subject was crucial to the literature review and thus the designing of the study; Dr Alemayehu Seyoum, the designated discussant of the draft report, whose critical inputs have helped in further improving this work; and the Department of Sociology, AAU, that rendered valuable service in establishing contact with local administrations in the field.

Last but not least, we are grateful to the Forum for Social Studies, for providing the grant for the whole of the study project; the FSS staff who were involved in managing and facilitating our work. In particular, we are indebted to Dr Taye Assefa, the Research and Publication Director, who was instrumental in planning the study, and Ato Ayalew Kebede, the able driver, who saw us through the whole fieldtrip itinerary.

Obviously, none of the above mentioned institutions and individuals is responsible for the views expressed in this work or for any omissions and errors; for these we, the authors, take full responsibility.

List of Illustrations

No.	Title	Page
Fig. 1	Map of Central Ethiopia Showing the Study Sites	8
Plate 1	The *aräqe* still and aräqe distillation	27
Plate 2	*Aräqe* distillation	28
Plate 3	Markets for *aräqe* ingredients	29
Plate 4	Inputs, outputs and means of transportation	30
Plate 5	*Aräqe* market and wholesalers manning their collection stalls	54
Plate 6	Aräqe market and wholesalers manning their collection stalls	55
Plate 7	Wholesalers distributing *Aräqe* in their hometowns	56
Plate 8	*Aräqe* taverns of varying standards - I	60
Plate 9	*Aräqe* taverns of varying standards - II	61

List of Tables

No.	Title	Page
Table 1	Major typologies of *aräqe* production	25
Table 2	Distribution of direct and indirect supportive roles of household members in *aräqe* production, by sex and age	32
Table 3	Estimated price of *aräqe* production implements by study site	33
Table 4	Estimated cost of *aräqe* production ingredients, by study site	34
Table 5	Estimated time requirement for major *aräqe* production tasks	35
Table 6	Estimate of percentage of *aräqe* producers and non-producers in the study localities	40
Table 7	Long distance and local *aräqe* trade routes from or in the study areas	52
Table 8	Estimates of current percentage distribution of adult population by site, sex, and *aräqe* consumption status	70

List of Boxes

No.	Title	Page
Box 1	The *Gïbt'o Aräqe* Scam	22
Box 2	*Aräqe* Production and Mate Selection	37
Box 3	The Case of Ayäleč Yïmänu's Family	38
Box 4	The Case of Wäyzäro Kälämäwärq	66
Box 5	Menelik, His Greek Merchant, and the Small Serving Glass	74
Box 6	The Consequence of Sudden Change in Drinking Habits	76
Box 7	Sliding Down the Liquor Ladder	83
Box 8	The Downward Spiral Caused by *Aräqe* Related Spending	87

List of Annexes

No.	Title	Page
Annex 1	Glossary of Local Terms	107
Annex 2	Alcohol Commodity Chains in Developing Nations	112
Annex 3	Distribution of FGDs and In-depth Interviews Conducted, by Study Site and Type of Participants/Interviewees	113
Annex 4	*Aräqe* Production and Fuel Wood Consumption in Arsi Nägälle	114
Annex 5	Alcohol-attributable DALYs by Disease Category and World Bank Region, 2001 (thousands of DALYs)	115
Annex 6	Characteristics of Adult Alcohol Consumption in Different Regions of the World 2000 (Population Weighted Averages)	116
Annex 7	Symbols Used for the Transliteration of Ethiopian Words	118

I. Introduction

1.1 Background

There is no singular explanation for Ethiopia's underdevelopment. Impediments on its progress are innumerable and multifaceted. These include: negative natural/physical factors such as its unfavorable location, land-lockedness, rugged terrain, erratic rainfall, chronic drought, and land-degradation; its long lasting institutional lacunae that include the well-known ambiguous property rights and tenure insecurity; its age-old political instability that often culminated in civil wars; the high growth rate of its population; its unfavorable balance of trade and overall economic backwardness; the HIV/AIDS epidemic. In addition to these impediments to development and wellbeing, a few negative social phenomena of relatively recent origin have begun eroding its human resource base and overstretching its limited social services. Such is the case with the galloping addiction to, and abuse of, substances, of which the most prominent are č'at and home-distilled alcohol; the spread of pornographic dens and gambling hangouts.

Yet, Ethiopian society, like many others in the developing world, has ignored the issue of substance abuse. Instead of addressing the issue, the Government, for instance, has passively encouraged the cultivation, marketing and consumption of č'at, because of its importance as a source of cash income to many farmers and its significance as a major foreign currency earner to the nation.

Äräqe, the subject of this study, is a ubiquitous feature of present day Ethiopian society – with the exception of the predominantly Muslim communities. Its production, marketing, and consumption are so widespread and so entrenched that the issue of illicitness is almost never raised. Throughout the fieldwork informing this study, its legality was not questioned even once – by ordinary folks, police officers and local administrators alike.

Äräqe is more than the alcoholic drink of choice for people living in rural and small towns of Ethiopia, and its popularity is on the rise even in the big towns and cities. Thanks to its qualities of divisibility, long shelf-life, portability, and high unit value, it is also an important commodity that is produced by, traded between, and consumed in most of the rural and urban areas of the country. Its negative effects notwithstanding, it is a major object of exchange that ties cities to their rural hinterlands and with one another, thus becoming an important component of the social fabric of the society. Thus, it is an important social fact that cannot be dismissed as a fringe phenomenon.

In spite of the substantial amount of äräqe that is distilled, traded, and consumed within the informal sector, and the important place it holds in the socioeconomic fabric of the society, no comprehensive study has to date been undertaken on its interrelated aspects and at a national level. The few studies that have been made so far are all on one or another aspect of *aräqe* and also focused on single areas. The three MA theses (Endalew 2008; Nejibe 2008; and Wolde 1999) are, respectively, on the socioeconomic impacts of *aräqe* production and consumption in Arsi Nägälle *Wäräda*, on impact of *aräqe* production on the degradation of woodland vegetation and emission of CO and percolated matter during distillation in Arsi Nägälle *Wäräda*, and on the contribution of *aräqe* production to urban informal sector employment and income in Assäla Town. Thus, not only are the studies limited in their scope, but also geographically restricted to only two *wärädas* of Oromia Regional State that are located close to each other and surrounded by rural areas with predominantly Muslim population.

1.2 Alcoholic Drinks: Origin, Classification and Nomenclature

Man's experience with alcoholic drinks goes at least as far back as the emergence of agriculture in the Fertile Crescent and China. For much of their history which is associated with agricultural surplus production and the concomitant emergence of a ruling elite, as well as their intoxicating power, alcoholic beverages have been treated with deference as special articles the consumption of which was restricted to particular categories of people and on special occasions (Room et al. 2002, 22).

Beverages made by fermenting cereals, fruits, and honey were the earliest alcoholic drinks known to man and the type that had already spread around the globe – save Australia, Oceania, and parts of North America – before contact with Europe was made some 500 years back. Distillation of alcohol, on the other hand, is of much recent origin having made its way to Europe through the Middle East around the 11th Century from its place of invention in China, and was introduced all over the world together with European imperial domination (Room *et al.* 2002, 21-22).

Both fermented and distilled beverages are respectively distinguished by their source: homebrewed versus industrially produced ones. Homebrewed beverages are also dubbed "traditional" even if they have been introduced from abroad and indigenized only a few decades back. The literature on alcoholic drinks distinguishes between two types, namely, fermented beverages such as beer, wine, and mead, on the one hand, and distilled beverages, on the other (Room *et al.* 2002, 21-22).

As one of the earliest and major centers of plant domestication, adoption, and development, the Ethiopian highlands must have had a long experience with fermenting alcoholic beverages that goes back to the beginnings of settled agricultural life (Diamond 1997; Reader 1998, 206-8; Acuda 1988 cited in Abebaw, Atalay, and Hanlon 2007). Up until the 20th Century, the traditional alcoholic drinks of the populace were fermented beverages such as *t'älla, koräfe, and borde* that are made from cereals and *gešo;* and *t'äj* that is brewed from fermented honey and *gešo* was consumed by members of the upper class. Distilled beverages, on the other hand, appear to be of relatively recent origin, in spite of their current popularity.

Aräqe is a traditional home-distilled beverage that is made from an assortment of cereals such as wheat, sorghum and maize, and has a high level of ethanol. In its original state it is pure spirit with a neutral taste and clear, colorless appearance. Only when laced with flavoring and coloring compounds such as *gïbt'o, kosso* flower, and honey, before, during, or after distillation, does it acquire a variety of positive tastes.

In order to put *aräqe* within perspective, the typology of *alcohol commodity chains in developing nations* worked out by Jernigan (cited in Room *et al.* 2002, 53-4) can be employed to advantage. On the bases of the kind of network of production and marketing processes that are employed, the model differentiates between the following four *types of commodity chains* for alcohol that arose in history but survive to this day: (1) *Traditional*, that is the tight and simple type as with traditional beer-making using locally grown grain for consumption at the point of production; (2) *Traditional industrial*, that is essentially the same as the traditional one other than that production is in local private or public hands, the commodity is exchanged for cash, and advertising is price and quality oriented; (3) *Peripheral "cosmopolitan" (neo-colonial)*, that is marked by production designs that are passed from colonial powers or trading partners to local hands, by importation of some types of alcoholic drinks, and distribution by colonial authorities or their assignees; and (4) *Globalized "marketing driven"* is the type in which production techniques and recipes are drawn from global or regional transnational producers, local raw materials are supplemented by globally sourced inputs, manufacturing that is local is under control of transnational companies, and distribution is underway by transnationals and their subsidiaries. (See Annex 2 for the complete typology).

It is obvious that the above typology consists of two "pure types" that are at the opposite ends of the spectrum with two "hybrids" in between. Hence, any alcohol production-marketing system in the developing world can be viewed as momentarily occupying a position between any two of the four types, at the same time as it gradually evolves in one or the other direction. On the basis of what has been learnt through this study, it is possible to consider the *aräqe* production-marketing system of today's Ethiopia as falling between the *traditional* and the *traditional industrial* types. Also, it is becoming less of the former and more of the latter type by the day.

It would be necessary to point out that the characterization in the foregoing paragraph is only as regards traditional Ethiopian *aräqe* in light of the typology of *alcohol commodity chains in developing nations*. However, in today's Ethiopia not just one, but multiple types of alcohol commodity chains are found operating simultaneously. From the *traditional* type such as that of the brewing of *t'älla* for family consumption by a woman who uses grain from her own fields, to that of the *globalized "marketing driven"* kind that includes the importation of fine liquor and wines designed and manufactured by global producers for the consumption of the affluent and the middle-class, operate side by side. Even the third form, the *peripheral "cosmopolitan" (neo-colonial)*, despite its label (that sounds oxymoronic in relation to independent Ethiopia), has operated in the country in spite of the nationalization onslaught it suffered following the outbreak of the Ethiopian Revolution. One can recall the famous brands of Elias Papasinos and Molla Marru, and many smaller ones whose recipe and production designs were passed to them from western colonial interests through middle-men and trading partners.

There are two names by which the home-distilled traditional alcoholic beverage is known in Ethiopia: *katikala* and *aräqe*. Both of these terms are loanwords of south Asian origin (*katikala* and *arrack*) that must have reached the country together with the product and its extraction technique via the Middle East. Although the more complete rendition of the latter term is *yä abäša aräqe*, which distinguishes it clearly from its industrially produced counterpart that goes by the name of *yä färänj aräqe* (literally, Whiteman's *aräqe*), the shorthand form, *aräqe*, is widely used as people understand by it the home-brewed and distilled stuff. On the other hand, while the term *aräqe* and *katikala* are interchangeably used in the country, the study has found the former to be the most dominant one in all of its study areas, and for this reason and this reason alone the term *aräqe* is employed throughout this paper.

1.3 Objectives

This study was originally envisaged as a study of "the socioeconomics of rural *aräqe*". According to this original plan, urban centers were meant to be investigated only to the extent they served as conduits of *aräqe* marketing. As the study progressed, however, it became very clear that urban centers of various sizes and status were inseparably linked to their immediate rural hinterlands and in some cases even to those that are very far away. This linkage pertained to the production, marketing, and consumption of *aräqe* in such a complex manner that it became clear that the study has to be on *aräqe* in the rural areas as well as the small and large urban centers whose hinterlands they form.

Accordingly, the general objective of this study is to assess and document the *processes* (origin, introduction and spread), *patterns* (arenas, manners), *trends* (currently evolving forms and future directions), as well as *impacts* (on environment, economy, social, health and security) of the *production, marketing,* and *consumption* of the homemade liquor, *aräqe,* with the ultimate aim of indicating how and to what extent these factors contribute to economic development/stagnation and social cohesion/disruption in rural Ethiopia in particular as well as the country at large.

The specific objectives of the study include, but are not limited to, assessing:

i. Processes through which, the production, marketing and consumption of *aräqe* was **introduced and spread** in the study areas —including factors that favored and impeded the process, possible struggle between contending actors, and the like.

ii. Arenas, manners, currently evolving forms, significance, as well as the impacts of *aräqe* **production and marketing** on the following:
   a. Locally available biomass and the environment;
   b. Household economy (including labor, cash in/out-flow, food security, and asset formation/depletion);
   c. Local economy (including employment opportunity, and contribution to various economic sectors);
   d. Women, children, and family.

iii. Arenas, patterns, currently evolving forms, significance, as well as the impacts of *aräqe* **consumption** with regard to the following:
   a. Household economy (including labor, cash in/out-flow, food security, asset formation/depletion);
   b. Women, children, and family;
   c. Local tradition, community solidarity and harmony, as well as community-based organizations and associations of reciprocity such as parish churches, *sänbäte, mahbär, ïdïr, jïge/däbo, ïqub* and the like;
   d. Health status of the population, and possible burden on health service;
   e. Personal/public security and crime/juvenile delinquency.

1.4 Method

The empirical section of the study is based on fieldwork conducted during the months of September and October 2009 in five sites: four rural *qäbäles* and two market towns and three town *qäbäles* that are geographically, economically and socially linked to them, as well as one urban center that plays a very special role in supplying near and distant areas in central, southern, and south-western

Ethiopia with *aräqe*. The four rural *qäbäles*, two market towns, three urban *qäbäles*, and two towns are found grouped in the five study sites, as follows:

i. Gorfo *Qäbäle* and Gorfo Market Town[1], and Dubär Town – Sululta *Wäräda;*

ii. Qäyït *Qäbäle* and Qäyït Market Town, Bassona Wärana *Wäräda*, and *Qäbäle* 02 of Däbrä Bïrhan Town;

iii. Yäšäboč *Qäbäle* and *Qäbäle* 02 of Dämbäč'a Town – Dämbäč'a *Wäräda*

iv. Yäfeq-T'äräq *Qäbäle* and *Qäbäle* 01 of Ïmdïbïr Town – Čäha *Wäräda;* and

v. Arsi Nägälle Town, which was included in the study due to its special position as a major *aräqe* production center that supplies many areas including some of those covered by this study.

The scope of the initial research design was limited to three distinct but interrelated case studies in three rural areas known for their *aräqe* production and consumption, namely, a *qäbäle* each from Däbrä Bïrhan, West-Gojjam, and Sululta-Dubär areas. However, based on the insight gained during the survey in these areas, it was found necessary to extend the study to Arsi Nägälle and Čäha-Ïmdïbïr.

Moreover, in accordance with its objectives and following its original design, the study has mainly focused on rural *qäbäles* but without losing sight of those urban centres that serve them as conduits. It ought to be mentioned, however, that the reality of the field has compelled the actual data collection activity to veer more towards the urban centres and their marketplaces than what was anticipated in the original study design as presented in the proposal.

The primary data collection methods employed, were the following:

a. *In-depth interview*: (1) with *aräqe* distillers, distiller-sellers, sellers, and their spouses and children, as well as *aräqe* bar-girls, retailers, persons engaged in cross-country wholesale, brokers/tasters, and transporters were mainly geared towards obtaining personal information pertaining to the interviewees' different involvements with *aräqe* and personal and family histories, (2) with key informants such as elders, traditional

---

[1] The term 'market town' here refers to points of small population agglomeration that have the characteristic features of urban centers in terms of non-agricultural occupation of the residents as well as density of population, but the size of which is below the 2,500 administrative cut-off point and are therefore not officially designated as city, town, or 'emerging town'.

leaders, local administrators, police officers, health workers, and the like, focusing on community-wide events, features and issues.

b. **_Focus group discussion/interview_**: with groups of: (1) women engaged in *aräqe* production and marketing, (2) community leaders, (3) male and female development extension workers, teachers and local NGO beneficiary committee members.

The FGDs were made to focus on, but not limited to, community-wide issues pertaining to *aräqe,* such as historical developments and timelines, old and current patterns, emerging trends, and general magnitudes, site-specific estimates (of *aräqe* production, sales/ purchases, and consumption) as well as their impacts.

Annex 3 gives the distribution of a total of 14 FGDs and 59 in-depth interviews that were actually conducted, by study site, urban and rural locations, and type of participants/ interviewees.

Fig. 1: Map of Central Ethiopia Showing the Study Sites

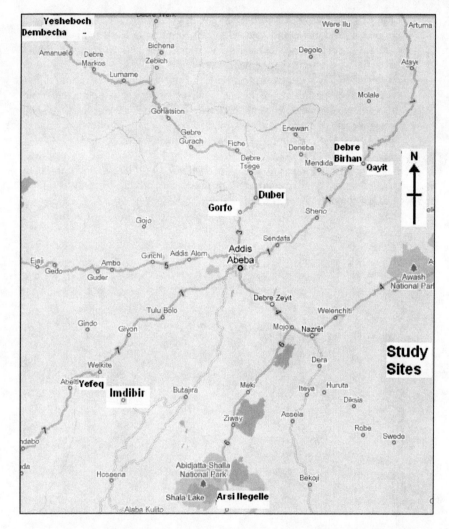

A category of persons that is arguably very important from the perspective of this research, but one that is conspicuous for its absence from the list that follows, is that of *aräqe* drinkers. However, a separate FGD with such a group was unnecessary due to the fact that many *aräqe* drinkers – by their own open admission – were present in force at most of the FGDs, and were always forthcoming and frank regarding the state and behavior of that category of people.

For the purpose of systematically obtaining comparable information from the various study sites, the following 11 in-depth interviews and focus-group discussion guides were employed:

i. Guide for focus group discussion with distillers and distiller-sellers
ii. Guide for focus group discussion with CBO leaders, spiritual leaders, teachers, local businessmen and businesswomen
iii. Guide for in-depth interview with distillers and distiller-sellers
iv. Guide for in-depth interview with husbands of distillers
v. Guide for in-depth interview with children of distillers or distillers-sellers
vi. Guide for in-depth interview with people that are engaged mainly in long-distance and/or local/fixed, wholesale and/or retail *aräqe* trading
vii. Guide for in-depth interview with elders
viii. Guide for focus group discussion with agriculture extension workers, health extension workers, microfinance extension workers, teachers, and NGO project staff and/or beneficiary's committee members
ix. Guide for in-depth interview with local health workers
x. Guide for in-depth interview with the local police
xi. Guide for in-depth interview with *wäräda* and *qäbäle* officials.

In addition to the above, available secondary data relevant to the study were gathered and analyzed. The major sources of the secondary data were the few official records obtained from the various government agencies in the study areas such as police stations, health centers, and *qäbäle* and *wäräda* administrations. Also, other studies such as the few fieldwork-based MA theses and other published materials have informed the study to some extent.

The field data by the two authors themselves who traveled to the sites and conducted all the FGDs and in-depth interviews together. Only for the purpose of facilitating our entrance into the fields and to help out with translation in those very few cases where Oromiffa and Amharic translation was required, were other persons used.

It is worth noting that the study was preceded by, and benefited from, exploratory queries that were undertaken in the early 1990s by the first author of this work. Taking advantage of a number of fieldworks that he conducted in the various parts of the Ethiopian highlands in conjunction with other social investigations, this researcher was able to collect information and gain insight into the magnitude and the nature of the problem which helped shape the conduct of the final study the findings of which are being reported here.

A word or two on how the postscript came to be added to this report is necessary here. After completion of the field work, the findings were first presented at a dissemination workshop in January 2010. By coincidence, Proclamation No. 661/2009 to Provide for Food, Medicine and Health Care Administration and Control was passed on 13 January 2010. Furthermore, 193 Member States of the World Health Organization (WHO) adopted the Global Strategy to Reduce the Harmful Use of Alcohol on 20 May 2010, creating an international convention on alcohol that will guide the policies and actions of individual countries for the first time ever. In Ethiopia, this was followed by the replacement of the old Drug Administration and Control Authority (DACA) by the Food, Medicine, Health Care Administration and Control Authority (FMHACA) on 9 July 2010. Cognizant of the changes in the legislative and institutional environment brought about by these recent developments, and taking advantage of the possibility of updating the study in order to bring its findings and recommendations into line with the changed circumstances, additional field- and desk-work was undertaken. This involved examining the relevant UN, WHO and FMHACA documents as well as conducting extended face-to-face and telephone interviews with the Deputy Director General of FMHACA, Ato Dawit Dikasso. The results of this latest effort are given in Section 7.2 and form the basis for the revision of Section 8.2.

1.5 Scope

Subject-wise, the scope of the study was limited to the generation of data aimed at creating a better understanding of the production, marketing, consumption patterns and trends of home-distilled *aräqe* as well as their significance and impacts at the household and community levels. Thus, the goal of the study was the identification, sketching, and understanding of patterns and trends. When it came to assessing the magnitude of the amounts of home-distilled *aräqe* that is produced, marketed, or consumed at any level, as well as that of the extent and seriousness of their effects, the study has only treaded carefully on the issue by soliciting informed estimates as their actual measurement was beyond its scope.

In many developing countries such as Ethiopia, ethno-religious variations account for differences in drinking norms and habits. In this regard, we ought to point out the fact that the geographical coverage of the study is limited to the mainly Christian central parts of the country and one more multi-ethnic and mainly Christian urban center in the South. This was done on purpose as the information that the study aimed at documenting and understanding could only be obtained and learnt from in areas where the practice of *aräqe* production and consumption is widespread.

We need to emphasize that this study is by and large about the livelihood of women and the conditions of women. As shown in the study, all of the *aräqe* that is produced in this country is distilled by women. Its production operation is also managed by women. Likewise, women are in charge of virtually the whole of the retail trade and most of the wholesale trade in *aräqe;* the only *aräqe*-related jobs that were found to be the special preserves of men were those of the professional taster and loader-broker, apparently due to the hazards that both of these occupations involve. For many poor women, and women of cash-poor areas, hitching themselves onto the *aräqe* business is usually the only course of action open to them.

Then, oddly enough, women who do not figure prominently in its consumption again appear as victims of its excessive drinking by men. The study does not include any special section on "gender aspects" or "gender matters" precisely because the study is in a sense almost all about gender relations as they relate to the *aräqe* phenomenon — a perspective that emerged naturally in the course of our attempts at documenting and understanding this important social fact and not so much by design.

II. Brief Profile of the Study Areas

Sululta *Wäräda* is located within the Finfine Zuria Special Zone of Oromia Region. Hence, its socio-economic structure and features are very much influenced by its proximity to, Addis Ababa. The two sites in the *Wäräda* on which the study focused, namely, Gorfo *Qäbäle* together with Gorfo Market Town and Dubär Town, being 45 and 65km away from Addis Ababa, respectively, and being located on the Addis Ababa-Däbrä Marqos highway, the economic and social interactions they have with Addis Ababa cannot be overstated. The *Wäräda*, particularly its rural hinterland, is inhabited predominantly by Christian Oromos. The total population of **Sululta** *Wäräda* is 129,322, of which the urban population (12,452) is almost equally divided between male and female, with the latter being slightly in the majority (Federal Democratic Republic of Ethiopia Population Census Commission 2008, 67).

Däbrä Bïrhan Town and Bassona Wärana *Wäräda* (which surrounds the town) of Amhara Region is a major economic hub for the whole North Shewa Zone of Amhara Region, while its relative proximity to Addis Ababa (130 km) has allowed it to benefit from closer economic and social ties with the latter. The rural areas and the small towns are Amhara and Christian, whereas Däbrä Bïrhan contains a small minority of Muslims as well as non-Amharas. The study focused on two data collection sites, namely, Qäyït *Qäbäle* together with Qäyït Market Town of Bassona Wärana *Wäräda*, which is only some 26 km away from Däbrä Bïrhan, and *Qäbäle* 02 of Däbrä Bïrhan town. Bassona Wärana *Wäräda* has a total population of 120,879. Of these, only 1,219 are urban dwellers among which 566 are males and 653 females. Däbrä Bïrhan town has a total population of 65,214 of which 31,658 are male and 33,556 are female (Federal Democratic Republic of Ethiopia Population Census Commission 2008, 62).

Dämbäč'a *Wäräda* of Eastern Gojjam Zone, Amhara Region, is located some 50 km from Däbrä Marqos town, 250 km from Bahïr-Dar, and 400 km from Addis Ababa. Its rural population is Amhara and Christian, whereas the town of Dämbäč'a boasts a small minority of Muslims. Its location on a major highway has consequences for its supply of *aräqe* to passing vehicles and bus riders, and must have contributed to its infamy as a capital of *aräqe* production. **Dämbäč'a** *Wäräda* has a total population of 129,228, of which 17,911 are urban dwellers with slightly over half of them being females (Federal Democratic Republic of Ethiopia Population Census Commission 2008, 63).

Čäha *Wäräda* of Gurage Zone, SNNP Region, drastically differs from the first four sites covered by the study on account of its primarily perennial cultivation. Households tend not only eucalyptus trees and *insät plants*, but also coffee and particularly *č'at* plants. As a result, there appears to be plenty of cash flow, coffee and *č'at* for direct household consumption and eucalyptus for fuel wood among other things. The profile of the area is remarkable for the nearly equal division of the population by religion: Muslims and Christians. This characteristic has given rise to a high consumption level of *aräqe* among the Christians, and that of *č'at* among both the Muslims and Christian youth. Čäha *Wäräda*, which has a total population of 167,745, of which only 6,588 are urban, has a peculiar distribution of its population by sex. Unlike the other *wärädas* covered by the study, a good majority of the rural population and a slight minority of the urban population are males (Federal Democratic Republic of Ethiopia Population Census Commission 2008, 76). This is certainly due to the well known tendency of Gurage men to migrate to far away places in search of work while leaving behind their women.

Socially speaking, Arsi Nägälle Town in Oromia Region is an island. Whereas the countryside is predominantly Muslim and Oromo, save for a few satellite market centers, the town is overwhelmingly Christian and home to people from different parts of the country. The town is well endowed with reliable pipe water supply and a large grain producing hinterland, in addition to being at a reasonable distance from a reliable source of firewood, viz., the Munessa-Šašämäne Forest Enterprise. It is also blessed with cheap migrant labor coming from the densely populated nearby Zones of Kämbata-T'embaro and Wälayta. Its location at the crossroads of Southern, Southwestern and Central Ethiopia is a crucial factor behind its emergence as an "*aräqe* capital" of that whole area. The town has a population of 52,329, of which 25,997 are male and 26,322 are female, slightly placing the latter in a majority (Federal Democratic Republic of Ethiopia Population Census Commission 2008, 71).

III. Introduction and Spread of Aräqe

Unlike the traditional fermented alcoholic beverages *t'älla* and *t'äj*[2], the distillation and consumption of *aräqe* by rural folks is a relatively recent development. Early travelers such as Alvarez that made reference to the consumption of *t'älla* and *t'äj* at the imperial court never mention any distilled beverages (Pankhurst 1965)[3]. Similarly, Pankhurst only makes note of the production and consumption of fermented alcoholic drinks and not of any distilled beverages in his *Social History of Ethiopia* (1990). An Ethiopian author by the name of Täklä Iyässus Waqjira, who lived during the reigns of Menelik, Iyasu, and Zäwditu, and wrote his eye-witness accounts as well as what have been communicated to him by others, makes mention of the consumption of what he refers to as *aräč'e* (ዐራጨ) and *t'äj* by members of the nobility and the clergy including church scribes and painters *(Aläqa* Täklä Iyässus 2002 EC. 83). Moreover, Jon Abbink in an Encyclopaedia Aethiopica entry on 'Drinks' positively states that, "...the distillation process, yielding strong liquor like aräqi, is a recent innovation, probably imported from abroad – or copied from resident Greeks or Armenians – during *Atse* Menelik II's reign" (2005, 199).

What was learnt in the field regarding the introduction of *aräqe* is in line with the above. The method by which *aräqe* is distilled is something that was definitely introduced into the country, including the areas covered by this study,

---

[2] The assertion concerning the relative recent introduction and spread of *aräqe* in Ethiopia might sound strange to members of the present generation. It is, we believe, possible to put this within historical context by considering the fact that even the longstanding consumption of *t'äj* was the preserve of the ruling class until the ban was lifted during the reign of Menelik II (Pankhurst 1990, 68 and 75). The following famous story shows how real the ban was. The story tells of a farmer who having collected a rich harvest got uppity to the extent of serving *t'äj* at his daughter's wedding, and was consequently flogged at the order of Emperor Yohannes IV.

[3] One cannot help wondering how it was possible that the Portuguese, who stayed in the country for almost a century (1548 – 1632), did not leave behind a culture of alcohol distillation as they did in other parts of the world to which they went at about the same time. For instance,

> The indigenous people of Brazil, to which the Portuguese first came in 1500, had various fermented alcoholic beverages, but the Portuguese introduced both wine and distilled beverages...; indeed, soon after the conquest production of a local distilled beverage called *cachaça* began, and remains important in Brazil to the present" (Room *et al* 2002, 23).

through a process of diffusion. This conclusion is borne by the identical nature of the method and the *still*[4] employed throughout the study sites and the country at large, the close similarity they have with those that are in use in many neighboring as well as distant lands, and, indirectly, by written history that makes no mention of *aräqe* production and consumption prior to the emergence of large-scale foreign trade and the coming of foreign businessmen, particularly Arabs, Indians, Greeks and Armenians beginning in the last decade of the 19th Century.

On the other hand, the fact that all of the component parts of the traditional still, save the metal canteen into which the final product drips and accumulates, are locally manufactured utensils of longstanding tradition that served other domestic purposes signifies the extent to which the externally introduced technique of distillation has been effectively indigenized. This indigenization has gone so far as to make its foreign origin difficult to trace, had it not been for the contrary telltale signs of the imported metal canteen and the two loanwords, *aräqe* and *katikala*, by which the product is interchangeably known to this day.

3.1 General Trends in the Amounts of *Aräqe* Produced, Marketed and Consumed

It was found difficult to establish with certainty the exact point in time at which *aräqe* began to be distilled in the study areas. Informants' recollection was found to be fuzzy, which could be due the fact that its introduction predates the lifespan of informants and also because informants were not in a position to know if and when *aräqe* distillation might have got a foothold in the homes of the resident pre-Revolution landed gentry.

On the contrary, informants were clear when it came to the times during which still processing became widespread and the vending and consumption of *aräqe* became common place in their respective localities. Marked differences, however, appear regarding informants' timing of the onset in the various study areas. There were general agreements among informants in Sululta and Čäha where absentee landlordism in prevailed until the land reform of 1975[5]. Prior to that event, *aräqe* consumption, while not completely unknown in the rural areas of the two *Wärädas*, was common only among the privileged few landowners in

---

[4] Technically, the term *still* is applied only to the vessel in which liquids are boiled during distillation, but the term is sometimes applied to the entire apparatus, including the *fractionating column*, the *condenser*, and the *receiver* in which the distillate is collected. The term *retort* is also sometimes used for a still (Davis 2006).

[5] The land reform following the Proclamation Providing for the Nationalization of Rural Lands and the Formation of Peasant Associations of 4 March 1975.

particular. Similarly, its production was limited to their households and a few petty distillers most of whom worked from the small towns or market places. In Däbrä Bïrhan and Dämbäč'a, on the other hand, no such linkage between the land reform and the spread of *aräqe* production and consumption was made by respondents. However, informants in all of the study sites generally agreed that prior to the 1950s/60s, the production and consumption of *aräqe* in the rural areas was very limited, if not totally nonexistent, and that it picked up with the increasing trend in the availability of cash in the hands of rural people. In this regard, informants in all of the study sites held the opinion that another clear leap in *aräqe* production and consumption occurred together with the market liberalization and the general increase in disposable assets that followed the EPRDF takeover power in 1991.

3.2 New Marketing Trends: Long-Distance Trade, Roadside Peddling, and Multiple Operations

Two relatively new developments have appeared in the marketing of *aräqe*. The first of these is long-distance trade in *aräqe*, which is a widespread phenomenon and one that affects the livelihood of a large number of people that play specialized roles. As long-distance trade is nowadays common in many parts of the country, differences exist between the long-distance trade systems as regards their: (i) trade volume or magnitude, (ii) type and parameter of catchment area, (iii) type and parameter/distance of destination area, and (iv) organization of specialists such as distiller-primary sellers, porter-brokers, tester-standard setters as well as middle men (local and cross-country wholesalers), vehicle owners, and drivers.

The second new development in *aräqe* marketing is roadside peddling to passing-by bus, minibus, and car riders. The practice is unique to the Dämbäč'a stretch of Bahïr Dar-Däbrä Marqos highway and affects a relatively small number of people. Here, girls and boys wave plastic and glass bottles refilled with *aräqe* often made by their mothers at passing-by vehicles and rush to sell it at negotiated price to interested occupants (see top picture in Plate 5). The practice is of quite recent origin, and appears to be closely associated with the rising popularity of the so-called *gïbt'o aräqe* that has brought fame to the area. It is noteworthy that the *aräqe* that is sold in this manner has a light tea-like appearance as it is laced with tea (see the reddish colored *aräqe* in the bottles held by the girls in the top picture of Plate 5) and continues to be sold to the unsuspecting passerby under the label of *"gïbt'o [6] aräqe"* in one of the most durable marketing gimmicks in the country.[7]

The retailing of *aräqe* in taverns that double as tea-rooms and eateries was also practiced in the towns. In exceptional cases, *aräqe-bets* are found attached to butcheries and haberdasheries as annex to the main establishment.

---

[6] *Lupinus albus,* commonly known as 'White Lupin', is a member of the genus *Lupinus* in the family *Fabaceae*. It is a leguminous plant usually cultivated as hedge, for erosion control or sometimes for human consumption.
http://www.henriettesherbal.com/eclectic/usdisp/lupinus.html
http://www.eol.org/pages/703662)

[7] On the basis of what has been learnt from informants regarding the *gïbt'o aräqe* that is peddled on the Bahïr Dar-Däbrä Marqos highway, we can deduce the following. Firstly, the need to continue with the bogus practice is a result of two interrelated factors that discourage the production of the genuine stuff, namely: the enormous trouble that *gïbt'o aräqe* production involves, on the one hand, and the limited demand for it at the place of origin on account of its extremely bitter taste, on the other. Secondly, the bogus practice was made possible and survives due to the peculiar nature of roadside peddling which is characterized by a fleeting vendor-customer interaction that makes confrontation and the settling of accounts unlikely.

IV. Aräqe Production

The production of alcoholic drinks is a longstanding human practice, with archaeological evidence showing that fermented beverages were used even among Neolithic people (Gaur 2006). In Ethiopia also, the production and consumption of alcoholic drinks has a long history. In fact, Acuda (1988, cited in Abebaw, Atalay, and Hanlon 2007) states that the mountainous areas of Ethiopia were among the first seven centers in the world where plants were grown for alcohol production.

Since its early beginning, the production of alcoholic beverages has spread to almost all corners of the world (SIRC 1998, 8). Through the years, most developed countries have managed to bring the production of alcoholic drinks under state supervision, thus standardizing the production process, inputs, as well as the concentration of alcohol (WHO 2004). However, in many countries in the developing world, particularly Africa, alcoholic beverages are produced traditionally at the homestead (Morris et al. 2006; Adelekan 2008) and provide the bulk of the alcohol consumed at the local level. Mesaki (1995, 138) argues that traditional alcoholic drinks of varying qualities and potency account for as much as 90% of the alcohol consumed.

Researchers focusing on traditional alcoholic drinks in developing countries maintain that homebrewed drinks fermented from cereal, fruits, and honey such as beers that go by various local names, some fruit-based beverages such as palm wine, and mead are common. Although of lesser magnitude, there are also a variety of home-distilled drinks made and consumed throughout the developing world (Adelekan 2008). While the fermented drinks have lower alcohol contents and short shelf-life, the distilled drinks are more potent and long-lasting (WHO 2004, 18). Furthermore, these studies have documented various traditionally brewed and distilled alcoholic beverages in developing countries, including *chang'aa* of Kenya, *bojalwa, khadi,* and *nyola* of Botswana, *burukutu* and *akpeteshie* of Ghana, and *kassippu* of Sri Lanka (Liyanage 2008), to mention some.

Home-fermented and distilled traditional alcoholic drinks are common in Ethiopia also where the two fermented beverages *t'älla* (the local beer) and *t'äj* have been consumed for a long period of time. Abebaw, Atalay and Hanlon (2007) explain that "*t'älla* is the most commonly home fermented alcoholic beverage ... and has an alcohol content of 2-4%. *T'äj* is a traditional wine made from fermented honey and *gešo* and contains 7-11% alcohol". In addition to these, we have *aräqe,* which is estimated to have an alcohol content of up to 45%[8].

In the sections that follow, we will focus on *aräqe* and look at the ingredients, implements and process of its production. Furthermore, we will discuss sources, types and combination of fuels used for *aräqe* production, labor requirements and arrangements, and the costs of *aräqe* production.

4.1 The Process of Production

Traditional *aräqe* distillation has certain discernable structures and patterns common to all areas and others specific to particular areas. It's been indigenized based on existing know-how, implements, and available resources. Through processes of social learning, experimentation, and progressive adaptation, best practices and methods have taken roots. The study has attempted to learn from these existing practices regarding the ingredients, implements, processes, fuels, labor requirements, and costs of *aräqe* production.

4.1.1 Ingredients, Implements, and Applications

As *aräqe* is a pure-grain alcoholic beverage, its production, involves the use of an assortment of cereals that are prepared in various forms to provide the natural sugar needed for fermentation. The second important input of *aräqe* is malt (*bïqïl*), which is obtained by steeping wheat in water and allowing it to germinate. A third ingredient that is common to all five study areas is *gešo* (shiny-leaf buckthorn, *Rhamnus prinoides; see bottom left picture in Plate 3*), which gives flavor to the *aräqe*. Of course, water is a vital element of *aräqe* production, used in almost every single step right up to the end.

The study sites exhibited important differences in terms of the ingredients used for *aräqe* production, particularly as regards the type of grain used and whether the malt is bought from the market or prepared at home.

While maize is used in Arsi Nägälle, Čäha and Dämbäč'a, a combination of maize and sorghum is used in Däbrä Bïrhan. Distillers in Č'anč'o, on the other hand, use wheat in combination with sorghum. The variation in the types of cereals used can largely be explained by the relative availability of the various grains in the particular areas.

Oddly enough, the study revealed that some distillers, especially in the rural areas of Č'anč'o, use the cheaper *ïnkürdad* (cockle, darnel, false wheat, *Lolium temulentum*) together with sorghum to prepare the *qit'a*. In fact, there used to be

---

[8] Note the total absence of any traditional fruit-based fermented or distilled alcoholic beverages in Ethiopia.

a trader in the locality whose sole occupation was the import of the cockle used for *aräqe* production. In the localities where this is practiced, it is popularly believed that, despite its greater potency, *aräqe* distilled from *inkïrdad* causes vomiting[9] and a severe headache when drunk[9].

In almost all of the study areas wheat that is already malted is bought from the market place and used (see bottom right picture in Plate 3). In exceptional circumstances, particularly in Dämbäč'a, the distillers themselves were found to do the malting process, which goes as follows: wheat or barley is soaked in water and kept overnight. The next day the soaked grain is washed and kept covered for three days, until it begins to germinate and the starchy interior of the grain is converted into maltose. On the third day the germinated grain is spread on a sheet and sun-dried, stopping it from germinating any further.

In addition to these common ingredients, other ingredient may be used in the making of flavored *aräqe*, such as *yä gïbt'o aräqe* (see Box 1) and *yä kosso aräqe, yä mar aräqe* (i.e., white lupin *aräqe*, hagenia *aräqe*, and honey *aräqe*, respectively).

---

[9] One source describes the consequences of consuming the grain as follows: "The symptoms are those of a deliriant nerve poison. There is confusion of sight which was known in very early times and is mentioned by classical writers. Further symptoms are dilation of pupils, giddiness, drowsiness, staggering and stupefaction. Trembling is followed in some cases by convulsions. In others vomiting and purging may take place. The respiration is labored and the pulse slow. Inflammation of stomach and intestine have been observed." (http://chestofbooks.com/flora-plants/weeds/Poisonous-Plants/Grass-Family-Gramineae-Darnel-Lolium-temulentum-L.html)

[9] This fact is universally recognized in the country as a whole, as capsulated by the lyrics of the song by the late Tilahun Gessesse that goes as follows:

> *Ïnkïrdad, ïnkïrdïd, yätänkärädädä*
> *Sïnde mäslo gäbto, säwïn assabädä. ....*
>
> (*Ïnkïrdad the rough, the roughed up*
> *Wormed its way pretending to be wheat, and drove people crazy.*)

Box 1: The *Gïbt'o Aräqe* Scam

> The most commonly peddled *aräqe* in Dämběcha is the so-called *yä gïbt'o aräqe*, which was found to be none other than normal *aräqe* colored with tea leaves. The study made an attempt to check the truthfulness of this matter by cross-checking information from community leaders, *aräqe* distilling women and other key informants. When asked if they produce *yä gïbt'o aräqe*, all of the distillers stated that they don't produce it, as processing *gïbt'o* involves a lot of work and the output is very small. Similarly, elders in the study community stated that a few women had tried to distill *yä gïbt'o aräqe* in the past but have given it up because it was too bitter and thus hardly palatable for many.
>
> All the aforementioned reasons are quite understandable because *gïbt'o* seeds contain strong bitter-tasting and toxic alkaloids. Thus, if *gïbt'o* is to be used for any form of human consumption, the seed should be thoroughly leached through repeated washing or extended soaking in water (http://www.pfaf.org/database/plants.php?Lupinus+albus+graecus).

The major implements of *aräqe* production include the various containers used for preparing the *t'ïnsïs* and *dïfdïf,* and the clay jar still itself. A plastic jar of 80 liters is the most frequently used material for preparing the *t'ïnsïs* and then the *dïfdïf*. It is also in this same container that the *dïfdïf* is kept for 4-9 days until it ferments. Sometimes, especially in rural parts of the study areas, a big clay jar is used in place of the plastic jar.

The traditional still is composed of the following major parts (see Plate 1): a clay jar in which the mash is boiled (*ïnsïra*), a small clay 'head cap'[10] (variously called *gït'am, qob, mädfia, dïffito*) which is used to seal the clay jar and connect it to the bamboo pipe around which a wet rope is coiled (*mässabia, šämbäqo, ašända),* and a metal canteen which is connected to the other end of the bamboo pipe and partially immersed in a clay, metal, or wooden bowl containing cold water (*wadiat, däqq, goras*).

In addition to the above listed implements, many other household appliances are used at various stages of *aräqe* production. Various containers for grain storage, plastic sheets on which grain and *gešo* are sun-dried, mortars and pestles to pound *gešo*, plastic bowls to prepare grain dough, water containers of varying sizes are all used for *aräqe* production.

---

[10] In Čäha the bamboo tube is connected directly to the clay jar and the link is sealed with *enset* bark soaked in dregs of *aräqe atäla*.

Despite the variation in their names, the implements of *aräqe* production are somewhat uniform in most of the study sites. An exception to this is Arsi Nägälle, where a relatively large-scale production of *aräqe* is carried out, demanding better implements to be used. One such implement is a larger and more durable metal barrel which is used in place of the plastic or clay jar used in other places. Similarly, improvements are made to the traditional still. First, the bottom of the clay jar is plated with a metal sheet which regulates the heat at the same time making it more long-lasting. Second, a wire is tied around the clay jars to fortify them against breaking. Finally, the *wadiat* is replaced by a long and narrow cement tub filled with water in which several canteens are immersed at a time.

4.1.2 Fermentation and Distillation

The process of *aräqe* production goes through three major stages, each of which involve various ingredients, techniques, and timelines. The first two stages, i.e., *mät'änsäs* and *mädäfdäf,* roughly correspond to the stage known as mashing in beer production. *Mät'änsäs* refers to the creation of a sort of starter mash (*t'ïnsïs*) which is usually a mixture of malt, *gešo,* and water. In rare cases, the *t'"ïnsïs* can be made only of *gešo* and water. The second stage, *mädäfdäf,* supplies the main mash to the *t'ïnsïs* in the form of cereal grains processed in different ways—resulting in the *dïfdïf.*

The third and final stage, distilling (*mawt'at-* literally *extracting*), is probably the only fairly uniform stage in the *aräqe* production process. The distillation of *aräqe* follows the technique normally known as batch distillation, wherein a mixture is distilled to separate it into its component fractions before the distillation still is again charged with more mixture and the process is repeated. In the case of *aräqe* production, the clay jar is filled with the *dïfdïf* and a slow constant fire is applied to the pot. This boils the mixture, forcing the alcohol (which has a lesser boiling point than water and is also less dense than water vapor) up. As the vapor escapes through the colder clay pipe and reaches the canteen immersed in water, it slowly condenses into a clear, colorless liquid and gathers in the canteen (see Plate 2). It takes about 2 - 2½ hours to distill a clay jar of *dïfdïf* into *aräqe.*

The above paragraph presents only a rough description of the *aräqe* production process. In order to appreciate the variation that exists among localities as well as among individual distillers in each locality, let's now turn to the distinctive ways according to which *aräqe* production is underway in the different study areas.

Sululta 1: First, the *t'ïnsïs* is prepared by mixing a significant proportion of the ground *gešo* (the plant is chopped into smaller pieces, dried and then pounded at home) with water, and keeping the mixture for one day. On the second day, the remaining *gešo* together with the malt (ground at the flour mill) is added to the *t'ïnsïs*. This is followed by immediately adding *qit'a*[11] (flat bread baked from wheat and sorghum flour) into the *t'ïnsïs*. The resulting *difdif* is kept in a closed container and left to ferment for *six* days. On the sixth day the fermented *difdif* is transferred, portion by portion, to a clay jar and distilled.

Sululta 2: A slightly different approach is followed by the second interviewee. Instead of preparing the *t'ïnsïs* in two steps, as described above, she prepares the *t'ïnsïs* by mixing the malt and *all* the ground *gešo* (the malt ground at the flour mill and the *gešo* pounded at home) with water, and keeping the mix for a day. On the next day, *qit'a* is baked and added to the *t'ïnsïs*, together with more water. The resulting *difdif* is kept in a closed container for nine days until it ferments, and on the ninth day it is distilled. It takes 2 - 2½ hours to distill a clay jar of *difdif* into *aräqe*.

Dämbäč'a: Distillers in Dämbäč'a prepare the malt needed for *aräqe* production by themselves, making it the first preparatory stage in the *aräqe* production process. Once the wheat or barley is malted, it is milled together with the *gešo*. The malt and *gešo* flour is then mixed with water in order to make the *t'ïnsïs* and fermented for *three to four days*. A different technique and input is used in making the *difdif* – which in the case of Dämbäč'a is based on *däräqot* rather than *qit'a*. *Däräqot* is maize which is soaked in water for three days, roasted, sun-dried and then milled. The *däräqot* is added to the *t'ïnsïs* and the resulting *difdif* is fermented for about four days. Finally the *aräqe* is distilled in a manner similar to the other localities.

Čäha 1: Distillers in rural Čäha add one more method of producing *aräqe*. The *gešo* is mixed with malt and ground. Maize flour, which is moistened with water, is kept for three days and stir-roasted on the third day. The resulting *ïnkuro* and the previously prepared flour of *gešo* and malt (a small amount of which is kept aside for later use) are added to water and allowed to ferment for three days. A small amount of malt flour is mixed with about a liter of water and boiled until it thickens. The result of this process, the *absit*, is added to the *difdif* to act as a fermenting agent, and the *difdif* is left to ferment for three more days. On the third day the *difdif* is distilled into *aräqe*.

Čäha 2: The study found still another variation in the *aräqe* production process in Čäha. First, the pounded *gešo* is mixed with water and kept for *three days*. On the third day, the malt flour is moistened with boiling water and left to cool. Once it cools down, it is added to the initial *t'ïnsïs* of *gešo* and water, completing the making of *t'ïnsïs*. This mixture is kept in a big clay jar for a day. On the next day, *ïnkuro* (prepared by lightly wetting maize flour and stir-roasting

---

[11] It also goes by the additional names of *dabbé* and *qäleto* in other places.

it right away and letting it cool down) is added to the *t'ïnsïs*. The resulting *dïfdïf* is left to ferment for three days. On the third day, the *dïfdïf* is thinned down with water. The next day the *dïfdïf* is distilled.

Arsi Nägälle: The typical *aräqe* production process in Arsi Nägälle goes as follows. Barley and *gešo* are mixed and powdered at the flour mill. The resulting flour is mixed with water and kept overnight in a closed container—giving the *t'ïnsïs*. The next stage, *mädäfdäf*, involves the addition of *ïnkuro* into the *t'ïnsïs*. *Ïnkuro* is prepared from maize flour which is moistened with water, kept overnight and stir-roasted. The *dïfdïf* is then left to ferment for four days. The distillation process follows the same general pattern described in the previous cases.

The above presentation reveals the existence of three major typologies of *aräqe* production —*qit'a* based, *däräqot* based, and *ïnkuro* based. Table 1 summarizes these typologies of production.

Table 1. Major typologies of *aräqe* production

Type	Cereal/s Used	Locality	Preparation
Qit'a-Based	Wheat / maize with sorghum	Sululta, Däbrä Bïrhan	Milled, made into a dough, and baked
Däräqot-Based	Maize	Dämbäč'a	Steeped, roasted, sun-dried, and milled
Ïnkuro-Based	Maize	Arsi Nägälle, Čäha	Milled, steeped, and stir-roasted

4.1.3 Sources, Types, and Combination of Fuels

Various products of the eucalyptus tree, i.e., split logs, dead branches, leaves and pods (seed capsules) meet the bulk of the fuel demand for *aräqe* production. In addition to these, distillers in the study sites were found to use dung, wood chips, and acacia and juniper wood at the different stages of the *aräqe* production process.

As can be seen from the discussion below, these fuels are obtained either from one's own source (such as own tree, dung from cattle owned by the family), collected from communal fuel resources or bought from wood merchants, who themselves obtain the fuels from different sources.

Respondents in Sululta stated that split eucalyptus wood is their major fuel used for *aräqe* production. Dung is additionally used as fuel, especially for the baking of *qit'a*. At the distillation stage, twigs/branches are used together with split wood. Though not as commonly as eucalyptus wood, acacia and juniper wood is also used as fuel. When asked where they get the fuel from, they explained that they buy it from fuel wood sellers. When further asked about where the fuel wood sellers get the eucalyptus, some interviewees responded by saying that they bring it from natural forests in neighboring *wärädas*, while others illegally cut trees from government plantation in the *Wäräda*. It was also stated that the fuel wood sellers sometimes sell fuel wood obtained from their own sources.

Distillers in Čäha, an area well known for the relative abundance of eucalyptus trees, were found to use split eucalyptus wood and eucalyptus leaves for the grain roasting as well as distilling stages of *aräqe* production. As can be expected, an investigation into the source of firewood revealed that almost all of the fuel used comes from eucalyptus trees planted for sale by people in the study locality and cut, split and sold at the homestead, by the roadside and at market places.

Once again, eucalyptus was found to be the fuel for *aräqe* production both in Däbrä Bïrhan and Dämbäč'a. Urban-based distillers in both localities buy the eucalyptus wood, leaves, and pods from people who collect/cut it from natural forests in the *Wäräda* or other neighboring *wärädas*. On the other hand, rural distillers in Däbrä Bïrhan supplement the fuel they buy from firewood sellers with dead branches, leaves and pods they themselves collect from the surrounding forest. Since most households in rural Dämbäč'a have a few eucalyptus trees around the homestead, they use the products (wood, leaves, and pods) of their own trees. It was also found out that distillers routinely collect firewood from the surrounding forest. Of course, dung is used along with the eucalyptus products in both localities, especially during the dry season where the dung is not rendered useless by the rains.

Arsi Nägälle hosts several fuel wood markets, brimming with a variety of wooden materials (see top picture in Plate 4). However, most of the fuel wood sold on the market is not of local origin. Since the voracious demand of *aräqe* production for fuel wood has effectively exhausted the available biomass in the hinterlands of Arsi Nägälle. The major sources of firewood are various zones in the SNNPR and neighboring *wärädas* of Arsi Nägälle. While eucalyptus logs are trucked in from Zones in SNNPR, imports of forest products from of the Munessa-Šašämäne Forest Enterprise (later renamed 'Arsi Forest Enterprise' and now under the Oromia Forest and Wildlife Authority) account for a bulk of the fuel consumed in the town. In addition to these, juniper wood cut (illegally) from the few remaining natural forest around the town is used.

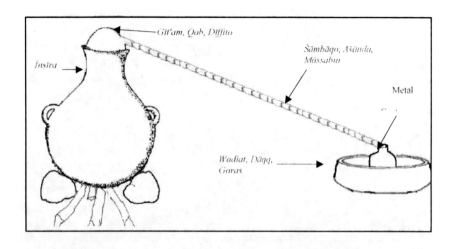

Plate 1: The *aräqe* still and aräqe distillation

Top: Sketch of a typical traditional Ethiopian *aräqe* still.

Bottom: An ordinary distillery using two stills simultaneously. Däbrä Bïrhan (Note the mash in the bucket at the bottom of the picture).

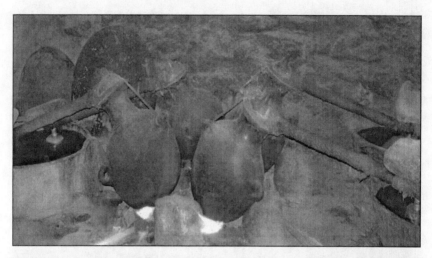

Plate 2: *Aräqe* **distillation**

Top: An ordinary distillery using four stills simultaneously.

Bottom: Improved stills at an advanced cottage distillery, Arsi Nägälle.

Plate 3: Markets for *aräqe* ingredients

Top: Arsi Nägälle's main grain market

Bottom Left: *Gesho* being sold at Däbrä Birhan Market

Bottom Right: Malt (*biqïl*) being readied for the market in Arsi Nägälle

Plate 4: Inputs, outputs and means of transportation

Top: Stacks of *aräqe* firewood and the makeshift wheelbarrow used to for its transportation, Arsi Nägälle

Bottom: A donkey cart used for in-town transportation of *aräqe* riding past an Isuzu truck that is waiting to be fully loaded with *aräqe* for a long distance ride to another town

4.1.4 Labor Requirements and Arrangements

Aräqe production is quite an arduous job which requires long hours of hard work at almost all stages of the production process. The multiple tasks of pounding grain and *gešo,* carrying grain/flour, fetching water, making *qit'a, ïnkuro, and däräqot,* mixing the various ingredients, and finally distilling the *aräqe* amount to several man-hours of work, all requiring careful execution if the *aräqe* produced is to be any good. Leaving the details to be discussed in the following section, let's now look at how this labor requirement is met and the arrangements involved.

The study found that the bulk of the labor requirement in the production of *aräqe,* particularly in Sululta and Čaha, is provided by the distillers themselves or the distillers and/or other members of their household (children, kin, and husbands). Even in those few instances where *aräqe* distilling is carried out by the distiller herself, without the direct participation of other household members in *aräqe* production, one cannot overstate the role of these other household members, since they support the primary distiller by carrying out other household chores such as child care, cooking, and cleaning. The same pattern was found among distillers in rural Dämbäč'a and Däbrä Bïrhan.

Table 2 gives the distribution of the supportive roles of household members in *aräqe* production, by sex and age, and with activities listed in the order of their importance.

As the production of *aräqe* becomes more export-oriented and large-scale, as is the case in urban Dämbäč'a and urban Däbrä Bïrhan, hired hands begin to involve at various stages of the production process. Interviews with distillers in these two study sites revealed two major employment arrangements. On the one hand, there are the live-in maids who are paid on a monthly basis. They could be employed primarily to assist in *aräqe* production but may do other household chores also, or primarily for household chores but also spend a significant proportion of their time on *aräqe* production. On the other hand, we find the various laborers employed to do an assortment of tasks (to split wood; to carry cereals from the market place, to and from the flourmill; and to roast the cereal or bake the *qit'a*) and paid as per the job they have done.

The use of specialized employed labor is a peculiar feature of *aräqe* production in Arsi Nägälle, where it has gradually evolved to the status of cottage industry. In fact, a person who owns a distilling establishment, and, therefore, manages and supervises production is generally referred to by the Amharic term *aswäč'i (አስወጭ),* whereas the word *awč'i (አወጭ)* signifies the distilling worker. Laborers are employed mainly for the two major tasks of preparing *ïnkuro* and distilling. This is mainly a result of the fact that most ingredients come ready-made, eliminating the need to employ someone to do them, for instance, wood is sold split, malt is bought from specialized malt makers, and *gešo* is ground at the flour mill.

An important that can be drawn here it that in Arsi Nägälle, *aräqe* production has evolved from a small scale domestic activity undertaken in a modified home environment to at least a medium cottage industry that is undertaken in a separate space, albeit on premises.

Table 2. Distribution of direct and indirect supportive roles of household members in *aräqe* production, by sex and age

Members	Direct support through labor contribution to *aräqe* production- related activities		Indirect support through labor contribution to other household chores	
	Male	Female	Male	Female
Adults	Husbands: - Split firewood - Cut down firewood - Fetch water - Get cereals and *gešo* ground	Female Kin: - Help in the making of *qit'a/däräqot/ïnkuro* - *Mät'änsäs* - *Mädäfdäf* - Distilling	Husbands: --	Female Kin: - Cooking - Cleaning
Children	Sons: - Collect fire wood/dung - Fetch water - Split wood	Daughters: - Clean implements - Fetch water - Collect fire wood/dung	Sons: - Herd cattle - Take care of younger siblings	Daughters: - Take care of younger siblings - Cleaning - Cooking

4.1.5 Costs of Production

In calculating the cost of *aräqe* production, we need to take into account not only the price of the items that go into the *aräqe* mash, but also the implements used for production as well as the cost of labor (both the labor-time of distillers and the wages paid for employed workers). The subsections below deal with these major categories of costs.

Cost of Implements: The capital goods of *aräqe* production and their corresponding prices as stated by different respondents are presented in Table 3. The table shows that there is a variation in the total price of these goods. One factor explaining this variation is the use of a big clay jar (*gan*), a plastic jar or a metal barrel for keeping the *aräqe* mash. Distillers in rural parts of the study sites, such as Yäfeq T'äräq of Čäha and Yäšäboč of Dämbäč'a, where production is still traditional, were found to use the cheaper *gan*. On the other hand, large-scale and export-oriented producers in Däbrä Bïrhan and Arsi Nägälle make use of the durable and more expensive metal barrel. Medium-scale producers commonly use the plastic jar.

Table 3. Estimated price of *aräqe* production implements, by study site

Site	Item									Total Price (birr)
	Plastic jar	Clay Jar (big)	Metal barrel	Clay jar	Clay head cap	Bamboo pipe	Steel canteen	Clay bowl	*Matot*[§]	
Čanč'o 1	180	NAP	NAP	15	2	10	45	10	NAP	262
Čanč'o 2	200	NAP	NAP	10	3	8	30	8	NAP	259
Čäha 1	NAP*	25	NAP	12	NAP	3.5	80	5	NAP	126
Čäha 2	NAP	50	NAP	5	3	4	60	4	4	130
D/Bïrhan 1	260	NAP	NAP	10	3	2	50	10	NAP	335
D/Bïrhan 2	250	NAP	NAP	13	3	3	45	15	NAP	329
D/Bïrhan 3	NAP	NAP	500	13	3	3	45	15	NAP	579
Dambač'a 1	250	NAP	NAP	12	3	0	50	12	NAP	327
Dambač'a 2	NAP	87	NAP	12	2	0	40	9	NAP	150
Dambač'a 3	200	NAP	NAP	15	1.5	0	50	15	NAP	282
Average	223.3	54.0	500.0	11.7	2.6	3.4	49.5	10.3	4.0	277.8

*NAP: Not applicable since the implement is not used in that particular case.
§ A circular seat for the large clay jar, made from *ïnsät* (false banana) leaves/bark.

An attempt was also made to find out the reason behind the difference between the prices of one product stated by different respondents. The most frequently provided explanation is variation in time of purchase, and thus price of items. This is particularly true of the steel canteen, the price of which varies significantly from time to time.

It is important to note here that the capital investment of *aräqe* production is small, i.e., equivalent to the value of a medium-sized ruminant or 25 Kg of *teff*, making it a choice occupation for the many, otherwise unaffording, rural and urban women.

Cost of Ingredients: As already described in Section 4.1.1, the major ingredients of *aräqe* production are the variety of cereals used to make the mash, *gešo*, and water. Table 4 presents the amount of *aräqe* that is usually produced at a time by distillers together with the amount of ingredients used.

Once again, we notice that not only the amounts but also the units of measurement of inputs and the amount of *aräqe* produced at a time vary across study sites. Variations aside, we can observe from the table that it takes about 2.5 Kg of cereals and 11.72 liters of water, on the average, to produce just one liter of *aräqe*.

Table 4. Estimated cost of *aräqe* production ingredients, by study site

Site	Amount and Price of Ingredient						Output
	Cereal		Gešo		Water		
	Amount (Kg)	Price (Birr)	Amount	Price (Birr)	Amount (Liters)	Price (Birr)	Amount (Liters)
Sululta 1 (Gorfo)	53.0	240	1/2 Sack	45.00	280	8.00	15.00
Sululta 2 (Gorfo)	56.0	230	30 Bowls	30.00	280	8.00	13.00
Čäha 1 (Yäfeq Täräq)	10.0	40	NAV*	3.00	53	0.10	3.33
Čäha 2 (Ïmdïbïr)	40.0	255	NAV	15.00	200	0.35	22.66
Däbrä Bïrhan 1 (Qäyït)	47.0	220	NAV	10.00	140	0.35	22.00
Däbrä Bïrhan 2 (Qäyït)	30.0	145	NAV	5.00	80	0.20	13.00
Däbrä Bïrhan 3 (Qäyït)	45.0	210	NAV	5.00	240	0.60	18.00
Dämbäč'a 1 (*Qäbäle* 02)	36.0	154	2 Kg	26.00	350	1.50	22.50
Dämbäč'a 2 (Yäšäboč)	36.0	145	2 Kg	30.00	122.5	NAP*	22.50
Dämbäč'a 3 (Yäšäboč)	40.8	165	2 Kg	30.00	122.5	NAP	22.50

*NAV: Unit of measurement *not available* or not known by respondents.
** NAP: Free water from spring.

Since most of the above-mentioned ingredients require processing and transportation, we have to take into account these costs, including those of grinding cereals at the flour mill, labor (making *qit'a/ïnkuro/däräqot*, porters), and fuel for processing the cereals as well as distilling the *aräqe*. The cost of getting cereals ground is about 15 cents per kilo (the *gešo* is milled together with the malt or pounded at home); the cost of labor ranges from 2-4 Birr paid for porters and men who split wood to about 10 Birr paid for the women who prepare the *qit'a, ïnkuro* or *däräqot*.

In calculating the cost of such traditional production schemes, the know-how and labor-time of the producers, in the current case the *aräqe* distilling women, need to be added to the material costs if a complete picture is to be obtained. The research made an attempt to take estimates of the latter at different study sites. Interviews conducted with distillers consistently revealed that *aräqe* production is a time consuming job. Particularly, the preparation of *qit'a/däräqot/ïnkuro* and distilling were stated to take anywhere between half a day to two days.

Table 5 presents estimates of the amount of time needed to complete the different tasks in *aräqe* production as stated by four distillers.

As can be seen from the table, *mawt'at* (distilling) takes the most time. Especially if the distillation is carried out one clay jar full of *dïfdïf* at a time (as is the case in most small-scale production schemes), which gives about 1.25 liter of *aräqe*, the process can take over two full days.

Table 5. Estimated time requirement for major *aräqe* production tasks

Site	Amount (Liters)	Estimated time in minutes						Total in hours
		Preparing the cereals and *Gešo*	*Mät'änsäs*	Preparing *qit'a/ däräqot/ ïnkuro*	*Mädäfdäf*	*Mawt'at* (Distilling)	*Total*	
Sululta 1	15	205	20	300	60	1620	2205	36.75
Čäha 1	3.33	180	NAP*	35	75	360	650	10.83
Dämbäč'a 1	22.5	165	90	305	60	540	1160	19.33
Dämbäč'a 3	22.5	180	120	480	30	960	1770	29.50

*Not applicable because the task is not done.

4.2 Significance of *Aräqe* Production

Production of traditional beverages provides a multitude of individuals and households with livelihood, either as the sole means of their sustenance or a source of critical supplemental income. Studies in various countries show that women are at the forefront of the production process and also benefit from the activity (Bennett *et al.,* 1998; WHO 2004). Many of these women not only benefit themselves through alcohol production, but they also support their families. In some cases the benefit goes beyond the individual and household levels to that of entire communities. Adelekan illustrates the situation as follows:

> In some rural African settings, a majority of women engage in the production and sale of these beverages as their main commercial activity and as a means of supporting their families. In some countries, homemade beer may be the most widely consumed alcohol and is quite significant in economic terms (Adelekan 2008, 3).

Our study has found that the production of *aräqe* is significant at the individual, household as well as the community levels in the study areas, in a manner similar to the situation described above by Adelekan.

As for gender roles in *aräqe* production, the situation in Ethiopia is peculiar in that all *aräqe* distillers are women, and men who themselves engage in *aräqe* distillation are almost nonexistent, as established by this study and other sources that do not make mention of male distillers[12] (see, for example, Nejibe 2008; Endalew 2008; and Wolde 1999).

4.2.1 Significance for the Producing Women

Aräqe production enables the producing women to generate cash income and therefore contribute to the household economy. Results of the FGDs and in-depth interviews conducted with *aräqe* distillers show that producing *aräqe* spares women the pain of asking their husbands for money day in and day out. Not only does this raise their self-esteem, but it also enhances their role as decision-makers on household issues.

For many female household heads and their dependents, *aräqe* production and sale is a niche that offers economic self-sufficiency. Together with brewing traditional fermented drinks, *aräqe* distillation is the major single source of

---

[12] This is not to deny the existence of some men who manage *aräqe* production establishments and direct the distillation operation that is carried out by women. One such exception is Ato Kassa Gämäču of Zwaï, who works together with his wife and other female workers, and whose produces have gained fame as far as Addis Ababa. (Unfortunately, Ato Kassa was unavailable for a direct face to face interview and we had therefore to do with a brief telephone interview with him, and information obtained through our common acquaintances, Ato Makonnen Yimam and Ato Abye Araya-Selassie.)

employment particularly for single women. Of course, the level of significance of *aräqe* production for the distillers varies from woman to woman. However, we can identify two broad categories of distillers on the basis of the significance of income from *aräqe* production. In the first category we find those women, usually married and with children, who use the income from *aräqe* production only as supplementary to income from other sources. Young unmarried women, middle-aged and older women who are separated, divorced, or widowed, along with a few married women constitute the category of distillers for whom income from *aräqe* production, supported by other supplementary activities, is the main means of livelihood.

As evidenced by findings from other African countries, tradition alcohol production serves as a source of employment for up to one-fifth of the labor force (Room *et al.* 2002, 71). Similarly, an ILO study quoted in the same source concludes that traditional alcohol production is the most important source of employment for women in African countries.

The significance of *aräqe* production goes beyond the financial gains made through its sale, as it also contributes to the meeting of societal expectations such as those related to mate selection. Box 2 illustrates the case in point.

Box 2: *Aräqe* Production and Mate Selection

> One interesting finding made by the study is the role of *aräqe* production and ownership of *aräqe* production implements in mate selection. In rural parts of Machakäl, East Gojjam, one of the major traditional criteria a prospective husband uses to select his future wife is *aräqe* production skill and the ownership of *aräqe* production implements, particularly a big plastic jar and a steel canteen!

4.2.2 Significance for the Producing Family as a Whole

Aräqe is rarely produced for own consumption. Rather, the production is aimed at wholesale distribution at the local markets, retail trade at the homestead or specialized taverns, or occasionally take-away sale to local consumers (note that those who buy *aräqe* from others and retail it are not included here).

Those who produce *aräqe* for wholesale distribution make a profit of 2.16 to 4.37 Birr per liter. Since the amount of *aräqe* produced at one production session commonly ranges from 13 to 22.5 liters[13], the minimum profit made is 28 Birr

---

[13] An exception to this is *aräqe* production in rural Čäha, wherein the minimum produced goes as low as about 3 liters.

and the maximum about 98 Birr. When we consider the fact that most distiller wholesalers produce *aräqe* at least once a week and some even up to seven times per month, it becomes apparent that *aräqe* production is an important source of cash income.

The shows that the contribution of *aräqe* production for the economy of the producing and wholesaling family is supplementary to other livelihood activities. Many maintained that money obtained from sale of *aräqe* is used to cover small but critical household purchases of consumables such as table salt, coffee, cooking oil, and lamp oil; school supplies; and the like.

However, the significance of income from *aräqe* wholesale is much higher for large-scale producer-wholesalers, such as those found in Arsi Nägälle and urban Däbrä Bïrhan. The case of Ayäleč Yïmänu, presented in Box 3, illustrates this fact very well.

Box 3: The Case of Ayäleč Yïmänu's Family

> Ayäleč Yïmänu is an *aräqe* distiller-wholesaler living in *Qäbäle* 02 of Däbrä Bïrhan city. She is married and has three children. According to her, the production and wholesale of *aräqe* is the primary source of livelihood for her family, while the money earned by her husband, a barber, supplements the household income.
>
> Ayäleč runs large-scale production of *aräqe* for wholesale, which goes all year round, even during holidays. Using 3,000 Birr worth of inputs per week, she distills a metal barrel full of *difdif* every day. While the sale of the *aräqe* produced this way is sold for about 4,000 Birr, and the sale of the *atäla* (residue used for cattle feed) covers the expenses for laborers and for getting the cereals ground.
>
> Obviously, the weekly profit of 1,000 Birr has gone a long way for Ayäleč and her family. She is a member of an *ïqub* (temporary rotating saving and credit association) through which she saves 300 Birr per week. While sending her eldest son to college, who has now graduated with a BA, she was able to save about 5,000 Birr. Currently, she is sending her second daughter to college, paying the expenses using money earned from *aräqe* production.
>
> Ayäleč is an active member of the Amhara Credit and Saving Association and has taken three loans of Birr 800, 2,500, 5,000, and paid off all. With the aim of shifting to other businesses such as livestock raising and processing food items, she has applied for more loans. She has now fulfilled the requirements for the loan (she got a design for her house and got it insured) and is waiting for the loan to be released.

The benefit of *aräqe* production for producer-retailers is higher, as they produce it themselves and therefore make that first leg of the profit made by producer-wholesalers, as well as the profit made by retailers.

The benefit of producing *aräqe* is not limited to money earned from the wholesale or retail of the *aräqe*. Equally significant is the use of the dregs (*atäla*) left after the distillation of *aräqe* as cow feed. Distillers, both small-scale and large-scale, own a few livestock (a couple of sheep, a milk cow or two, or an ox), which are often fed with the *aräqe atäla* together with other items. In Sululta, the milk produced by cows fed this way is sold for 4.35- 4.50 per liter. In Däbrä Bïrhan, sheep are fattened and sold, milk cows are kept and the milk consumed at home; in Arsi Nägälle oxen are fattened and sold for 8,000-15.000 Birr, usually to be slaughtered and sold by butcheries in the nearby towns of Hawassa and Šašämäne; and in Dämbäč'a milk cows fed with *aräqe atäla* produce milk which is consumed at home or converted to butter and sold at the market place.

In addition to being sources of cash income, the cows and oxen owned by *aräqe* producing families are sources of dung, sparing them the need to purchase it from others or spend hours every day collecting it from the grazing fields. Thus, the complementarity of *aräqe* production and livestock raising is complete.

Moreover, even if one doesn't own livestock, which is true only for a few urban distillers, the *aräqe atäla* doesn't go to waste. Rather, it is sold for 1.50-3 Birr per bucket or jerry can. Money from the sale of *aräqe atäla* is often used to cover small miscellaneous expenses related to *aräqe* production.

4.2.3 Significance for the Local Community

Since the production *aräqe* is a cottage-level business, its significance at the community level is not as much as it is for the household level. Nonetheless, it still stands to be one of the many livelihood strategies members of the study communities utilize. Table 6 presents rough estimates of the proportion of *aräqe* producing and non-producing households in the various study areas provided by their respective focus group members of community leaders.

The table shows that, on the average, slightly more than half of the households in the study areas engage in *aräqe* production, thus making it a significant livelihood activity. When we add to this number all other people who are engaged one way or another (selling ingredients, employed as laborers, running flour mills, etc.), the significance of *aräqe* production for the community/locality becomes apparent.

Table 6. Estimate of percentage of *aräqe* producers and non-producers in the study localities

Site	% of Non-producers	% of Producers
Dubär	84	16
Yäfeq T'äräq	75	25
Däbrä Bïrhan (*Qäbäle* 02)	67	33
Yäšäboč Mäqälam	25	75
Gorfo	25	75
Qäyït	10	90
Average	**48**	**52**

4.3 Impacts of Aräqe Production

Aräqe impacts on the physical environment and society in many important ways. The study has identified four major negative consequences of *aräqe* production that are dealt with in the sections that follow, namely: its impacts on the environment, particularly on vegetation and availability of biomass, on the availability of food grains, on the wellbeing and health of women and children, and on marital and family relations.

4.3.1 Aräqe and the Environment

According to an influential model developed by Cotton and Dunlap, the environment fulfills 'three competing functions' for human beings, namely, *supply depot, living space* and *waste repository* (Hannigan 2006, 18). The first function refers to its utility as the source of air, water, food, fiber, biomass, renewable and non-renewable raw material and energy, etc.; the second to its usefulness as provider of space for residence, work, social functions and recreation, as well as their attendant activities such as communication; and the third relates to the service it provides as liquid waste and garbage sink.

Like any other cultural artifact of significant magnitude, *aräqe* is closely tied to the environment – particularly that of its immediate surroundings – in more ways than one. Its production, in particular, relates to the environment through its functions of *supply depot*, being the source of its various ingredients and particularly the biomass that fuels it. *Aräqe* production, which is undertaken within residential places, impacts the environment's *living space* function.

Before proceeding any further, however, we might as well deal with two environmental issues that are both marginal. The first of these has to do with the fact that *aräqe* production does not appear to significantly impinge on the *living space* function of the environment. *Aräqe* production does not always compete with the most important household activity on the hearth, namely food preparation. In fact, the two activities can be supplementary since the same fireplace, and at times even the same fire, can be used for boiling the *aräqe* mash and boiling water for tea, for instance, literally side by side. The second point concerns the fact that *aräqe* production affects the environment very marginally as *waste repository*. This is because the production process ends up without leaving any tangible waste matter – save for pollutants released into the air – that need to be disposed of as garbage. The dregs remaining in the boiler after the spirit is extracted through distillation is a valuable byproduct that is used as cow feed by distillers who keep cows themselves or sold at a quite high price (see use of by-product under Section 4.2.2).[14]

4.3.2 Impact on Vegetation and the Availability of Biomass

Devegetation in developing countries on account of drugs can be caused in three ways: clearing of forest or vegetation, cultivation of drug producing plants, and processing of the harvested plants. The kind of environmental damage found in a country can be through producers growing the plants, processing the plants into drugs, or both (UNDCP 1995, 35). In Ethiopia, whereas the environmental damage resulting from *č'at* is of the first type (land clearance to make way for *č'at* planting), the degradation caused by *aräqe* is of the second type (devegetation in search of biomass for fuel).

Before discussing the impact of *aräqe* production on the biomass and the environment, we should note two important features of *aräqe*. The first, unique to *aräqe*, is the presence of distillation, which involves cooking the *aräqe* mash for hours. The second, by no means unique to *aräqe* production, is the use of the traditional open hearth (which constitutes three stones of a similar height over which the cooking jar is placed) that allows heat to escape into open air, wasting valuable fuel.

The combined impact of these two attributes on the environment is perhaps one of the hard-felt consequences of widespread *aräqe* production. With the

---

[14] *Aräqe* marketing further impacts important *living space* aspects of the environment, namely those of residential and entertainment places. Such is the case, for instance, with residences that double as taverns, which are treated in Chapter Five.

exception of Čäha and Dämbäč'a, which are endowed with eucalyptus trees, all other study sites have suffered significantly in terms of loss of biomass. Respondents in Sululta stressed that the widespread practice of cutting trees for firewood from the natural forest in the hinterland has significantly reduced the vegetation cover in the area. In fact, whatever fuel wood supplied to distillers in Sululta now comes from either from riverine natural forest to be found along the banks of tributaries of Mugär River or illegally cut from state reforestation enclaves. The study revealed a similar pattern in both urban and rural Däbrä Bïrhan, where participants reported widespread illegal cutting of trees by fuel wood suppliers. The situation is even worse in Arsi Nägälle, where the land around the city has been cleared of almost all vegetation, necessitating the import of firewood from other localities. (See Annex 4 for details).

Not only are the trees or their branches cut for firewood, the forest bed itself is swept by fuel wood suppliers, usually poor women, for the eucalyptus pods and leaves, depriving the ground of any humus. The same can be said regarding the extensive use of dung as cooking fuel in rural parts of most of the study sites. This last problem was repeatedly raised by agricultural development agents, who complained that people do not spare even a small amount of dung to be used as organic fertilizer.

4.3.3 Impact on Availability of Food Grains

In Section 4.1, it is shown that large amounts of important food grains such as maize, sorghum, wheat, and barley are fermented and distilled to produce *aräqe*. Considering the fact that it takes about 2.5 Kg of cereals, on the average, to produce just one liter of *aräqe*, and relating this to the total amount of *aräqe* that is produced and consumed in the country, it is not difficult to estimate the total amount of the food grains "diverted" to *aräqe* production.

As an example, let's take a look at the impact of *aräqe* production on the availability of grains in Arsi Nägälle. In order to produce the 32,240,000 liters of *aräqe* "exported" from this town every year, it would take 806,000 quintals of maize and wheat. At the generous rate of two quintals per person per annum, this would have met the grain food requirement (or 75% of the total food requirement) of 403,000 people or 80,600 families of five persons. Extrapolating this to the nation, whose total amount of *aräqe* production we don't know exactly, we can get a sense of the missed out opportunity in terms of food security.

In addition, we ought to bring to the attention of the reader one indirect negative contribution of *aräqe* production on availability of food grains, namely, through replacement. Farmlands that were once used to grow food grains now grow *gešo*, thanks to the rising demand for fermented beverages and *aräqe*. This observation is supported by the findings of similar research on the impact of traditional alcoholic beverages in other developing countries. Mesaki (1995, 139), for example, documents a more extreme case where people, in response to the greater demand for traditional alcohol, have resorted to the planting of a type of bamboo, the sap of which can be used to make alcoholic drinks, instead of the maize they cultivated for food[15].

4.3.4 Impact on the Health and Wellbeing of Producer-Women

The human cost of *aräqe* production is hardest on the primary producer-woman. Focus group discussions and in-depth interviews conducted with the distilling women as well as other members of the study communities invariably revealed that too much and tiresome work is one of the major problems of *aräqe* production. As shown in Section 4.1.4, hours of work involving heavy lifting and other burdensome activities are carried out at various stages of the *aräqe* production process. Extreme exhaustion, sleep deprivation, and weight loss are all complaints made by distilling women which seem to be the direct consequences of the long hours of hard work done by distillers.

Apart from these direct consequences, it is noteworthy to take into account the indirect/opportunity costs. The first category of opportunity costs are those relating to distilling women's inability to participate and benefit from development efforts. While health extension agents complain about the fact that women who are engaged in *aräqe* distillation fail to follow instruction regarding child care, contraceptive use, sanitation, and child vaccination, and attribute this to the busy schedule of distillers as well as the tendency to focus on planning and executing the production of *aräqe*. Lack of time and/or energy to perform other household chores and failure to take care of children make up the second category of opportunity costs. Many *aräqe* distilling women complain that they don't have enough time to tidy up the home or do other chores. Some even stated that they often fail to cook for their children; instead, they feed them the *qit'a* baked for the *aräqe* mash or whole-boiled wheat (*nifro*).

Once again, let's return to the issue of the use of biomass fuel in primitive three-stone hearths. First of all, biomass is known to contain a large number of pollutants such as particulate matter, carbon monoxide, nitrogen dioxide, sulfur oxides, formaldehyde, and polycyclic organic matter, including carcinogens such

---

[15] The same author quotes Heise (1991) who states that in Cameroon "it is estimated that as much as one-third of the millet and sorghum harvest is diverted to manufacturing traditional beer, a practice which can lead to severe shortages between harvests" (cited in Mesaki 1995, 139).

asbenzopyrene and benzene (Ezzati and Kammen 2002, 1). Second, the burning of biomass fuel on open hearth or traditional mud stove in windowless and chimneyless kitchens results in high levels of indoor air pollution, as the fuel that is used is not completely burnt and the smoke created is not vented out. Our own direct observation of the kitchens in which *aräqe* is distilled confirms the intolerably high level of smoke and particulate matter and the suffocation it causes.

Nejibe Mohammed's study based on actual measurement of indoor air quality among *aräqe* distillers of Arsi Nägälle further shows that *aräqe* distillers are exposed to levels of CO much higher (90 PPM CO for 15 minutes and 10 PPM CO for 10 hours) than that which is stipulated by WHO as being the maximum tolerable for a healthy living (115.31 PPM CO for 15 minutes and 75.25 PPM CO for 10 hours) (Nejibe 2008, 52-59).

Most of the health problems reported by *aräqe* distillers as well as health care providers correlate with what the available literature presents as the health consequences of indoor air pollution. Acute respiratory infections of various sorts, chronic obstructive pulmonary diseases, eye problems such as cataracts and soreness, acute headache, and skin allergic reactions were all found to be diseases suffered by distillers to varying degrees. It is worth mentioning here that declining eye site and persistent cough were stated as serious health problems experienced by distillers across the study sites.

The use of open hearths and traditional mud stoves also increases the risk of burns. In Sululta for instance, three burn accidents suffered by distillers were reported by healthcare providers. Similar incidents are reported by FGD participants in Däbrä Bïrhan and Dämbäč'a.

4.3.5 Impact on the Health and Wellbeing of Children

The production of *aräqe* also jeopardizes the wellbeing of children. In regard to exposure to air pollution from biomass fuel, younger children who spend a large proportion of their time indoors, where there is a higher concentration of pollutants, together with or on their mothers' backs, are the most vulnerable victims. The suffering of young children doesn't stop here, however. Cases of babies who were left unattended and crawled into fire, hot *atäla*, hot ash, and drank large quantities of *aräqe* were all reported to have occurred more than once in the study sites. Though to a lesser degree, older children, who are almost always expected to assist their mothers directly in the *aräqe* production process, are also exposed to harmful pollutants resulting from the indoor use of biomass fuels. These same children also assist in carrying out other household chores, thus carrying increase workloads as compared to other children of the same age.

4.3.6 Impact on Marital Relation and Family Stability

The findings of the study indicate the existence of a rather smooth relationship among members of *aräqe* distilling families, as far as its production is concerned. Almost all of the still married respondent *aräqe* distilling women and their husbands reported the prevalence of mutual consideration and support when it came to undertaking the various tasks involved. The finding could, however, at least partially be due to the fact that the interviews were conducted with and on a self-select group, namely, couples that have managed to get over their differences and stuck together, and not with and on those whose disagreements have led to the dissolution of their marriages.

Moreover, this is not to say that life in *aräqe* distilling families is completely trouble free. Like all other families, they too have their share of friction even as they go about the production of *aräqe*. But the problems that crop up between family members in connection with their *aräqe* production activities are few and far between. These problems are such as those that crop up when children refuse to perform certain tasks, complaining of too much workload; or the ones that occur between household heads on account of mutual incrimination concerning the misuse of resources.

V. Aräqe Marketing

Until the intensification of trade and sustained urban development beginning in the last quarter of the 19th Century, not only the production but also the consumption of fermented traditional beverages, namely, *t'älla, koräfe, borde* as well as *t'äj* was a domestic affair throughout Ethiopia. Fermented drinks were brewed in the homes of people of all standing for domestic use by the family itself or to be shared with kin, neighbors, or followers on special social occasions. In those days, production and consumption were ordinarily not mediated by the market.

The case with *aräqe* is quite different in this regard. *Aräqe* appears to have been commodified from the very beginning of its introduction into the country that coincided both in space and time with the peaking up of trade and urban development. This is not, of course, to say that all *aräqe* that was distilled was destined for the market. People made, and continue to make, *aräqe* for their domestic use, but generally speaking, the bulk of *aräqe* is produced in Ethiopia for its exchange value and not to be used directly by the producers.

Another socio-economically remarkable aspect of *aräqe* marketing is its requirement for specialized spaces. Unlike its production that can be, and usually is, undertaken within the home or a modified home environment, the wholesale of *aräqe* and the sale of its allied ingredients, inputs, and implements require special spaces—market palaces. Even its retailing, which is sometimes underway within the home of *aräqe* distillers and/or retailers, its marketing drastically transforms the residential characteristic of the home albeit for the duration of its use as a tavern, as it becomes open to strangers acquiring some of the features of a public place.

5.1 Wholesale Trade

Thanks to the special qualities of *aräqe* as a commodity, viz. its divisibility, long shelf-life, portability, and high unit value, not to mention its relatively uniform taste and color that make possible the evaluation and scaling of its quality at different locations, it can be collected from small deliveries, moved around in bulk, and then distributed in smaller amounts. In sum, its very nature has made *aräqe* a suitable object of wholesale trade.

5.1.1 Wholesale Trade in Rural and Urban Settings

Sociologically speaking, the determination of a community or area as rural or urban is a function of its size, density, and heterogeneity of population that are all closely linked to the occupation of the totality of its residents – i.e., agricultural versus non-agricultural pursuit (Wirth 1938). Countries, however, adopt different numerical thresholds for the purpose of differentiating between their territories either as urban or rural. In Ethiopia, communities (actually, points of population concentration) the size of which is above 2,500 qualify for the status of urban center irrespective of their administrative function. However, in this study, we consider two rural market towns (that of Qäyït and Gorfo) as small urban centers due to the fact that they fulfill the function of urban center such as serving as market centers and, above all, since they house large proportions of non-agriculturalists.

Aräqe is marketed both in the rural and urban areas of all study sites save Arsi Nägälle, where it is produced and marketed only in the town itself and a few nearby market centers due to the preponderance of Muslims in the surrounding rural areas. In the rest of the study sites, on the other hand, while the urban centers figure prominently in both wholesale and retail *aräqe* trading, no wholesale trading activity takes place in the rural areas. Here, rural women who distil their own *aräqe* (as in the surrounding areas of Däbrä Bïrhan, Dämbäč'a, and Ïmdïbïr) or purchase it from urban-based wholesalers in plastic jerry cans of 1-5 liters (as in Sululta), retail it in their homes which periodically serve the purpose of *aräqe bet*.

The open markets in the towns of Dubär, Gorfo, Qäyït, Däbrä Bïrhan, Dämbäč'a, Ïmdïbïr, and Arsi Nägälle, are focal points of *aräqe* marketing. The open markets in all of these towns, save Arsi Nägälle, are bi-weekly markets where *aräqe* sellers and buyers from within the towns themselves, the surrounding rural areas, and in some cases even from nearby and distant urban centers congregate. The open markets house special sections where *aräqe* and its allied commodities including ingredients and inputs such as *aräqe* grains, malt, shiny-leaf buckthorn (*gešo*), aromatic woods, and firewood, as well as production and marketing apparatus such as clay jars, bamboo pipes, clay bawls, clay head-cup, plastic jars, jerry cans, and plastic water bottles are sold. The open market of Arsi Nägälle is peculiar in that it is overwhelmingly dominated by trade in *aräqe* and it is augmented by separate sub-markets specializing in *aräqe* grains, malt, and firewood.

The traders that operate in the different markets could be both locals and outsiders. On market days, long distance *aräqe* traders are to be seen as they man their respective collection posts and making purchases on their own or with the help of agents — tasting deliveries, negotiating prices, making payments, and getting their purchases poured into their large plastic jerry cans, and getting them loaded onto contracted open trucks or busses (see Plates 5-7). The long distance traders operate as purchasers-collectors in those towns they travel to on market days in order to bring their supply and then as sellers-distributors in their home towns to which they return with their purchases. As they make their purchases, they directly pour the *aräqe* that is delivered to them in small plastic jerry cans into their larger plastic jerry cans; later on, as they make their sales, they place their large jerry cans high on sorts of wooden beds from which they siphon out the *aräqe* pouring it into the smaller plastic jerry cans and water-bottles of the retail traders and consumers (see Plate 7).

Of the towns that are covered by this study, Däbrä Bïrhan, Arsi Nägälle, and Dämbäč'a serve as hubs of *aräqe* "export"[16] trade, while Dubär and Gorfo (as well as other towns outside the specific study areas, such as Č'anč'o, Č'äffe, Arb Gäbäya, Šäno, Aleltu, Gumär, Addis Ababa, Moyale, Gambella, and many more) serve the same purpose for its "importation", retailing and distribution into their respective hinterlands.

At the bigger *aräqe* marketplaces of Däbrä Bïrhan and Arsi Nägälle, it is common to see from a single vantage point three or more Isuzu trucks loading huge jerry cans of *aräqe*. In the smaller market towns of Dubär, Gorfo, and Dämbäč'a that also act as hubs of long distance *aräqe* trading, one sees long lines of large plastic jerry cans ranging along bus stops and inside bus terminals, inside the closures of taverns, restaurants, and, of course, at their marketplaces on market days.

Däbrä Bïrhan and Arsi Nägälle, the two largest towns covered by the study, also boast the two largest open markets in all of the study areas where *aräqe* is traded in bulk during every day of the week and hour of the day, albeit with varying degrees of intensity. As a result, both marketplaces have organized groups of young men that serve as porters-cum-brokers (see Plate 4). The municipal administrations of these towns have found it wise to help the regular hangers-on of their respective marketplaces to band together in officially recognized service giving organizations with clear membership, rights, and responsibilities such as helping in keeping the peace, order, and hygiene of the marketplace. In Däbrä Bïrhan, members of the brokers and porters organization would be seen collecting fines (for which they issue receipts) from market visitors who are caught relieving themselves in public, for instance.

The porters and brokers association of Arsi Nägälle *aräqe* market is superior to those of the other sites in terms of: (1) its size —with 54 regular members, (2) its longevity —having been in existence for over a decade, and (3) more importantly, as regards its level of organization —as indicated by the fact that the organization charges a fixed fee of 3 Birr for brokering and loading an 80-litter jerry cans, over and above catering to the needs and welfare of its membership, also supports 19 orphaned students by regularly providing them with school

---

[16] For lack of better words, the terms 'export' and 'import' are used in this paper to respectively refer to *aräqe* that is sent to, and received in, other localities within the country.

supplies. According to informants, one previous member of the organization has gone as far as graduating from a law school and acceding to the bench; and a second who has also graduated with a law degree and practices law, had the good fortune of representing his old organization in a court case.

The *aräqe* marketplace of Arsi Nägälle, exceptional as it is always, is also unique in that it has some 150-200 non-organized individuals who serve as *aräqe*-tasters. It is common to see these individuals wandering from one buyer's stall to another to which they are called for their service.

In all *aräqe* marketplaces of the study sites, the quality of each and every delivery of *aräqe* is assessed and categorized as prime, second-rate, and poor on the basis of its *appearance* as well as its *taste*. Thus, firstly, professional tasters or the purchasers themselves fill up a transparent bottle with a sample of the delivery which they then shake vigorously to check if it still keeps its transparent color and also see if foams that stick around the inside of the bottle's neck in beads-like formation are generated by the action, which is taken as proof of high grade product[17].

Secondly, the professional tasters or the purchasers themselves take a gulp of the sample, role it in their mouths, spit it out, and pronounce their final verdict. The third-rate *aräqe* is variously known as *kolombia* in Sululta, *boche* in Arsi Nägälle, and *šäratä* in Dämbäč'a; and fetches some 4 Birr less per liter, on average, as compared to the prime stuff.

The value of a product, such as home-distilled alcohol that is non-standardized and non-certified, also depreciates in value in direct proportion to the distance it travels until it reaches its final market destination. In Gorfo and Dubär, for instance, other things remaining equal, the highest prized *aräqe* is the one originating from the nearby Č'anč'o Town, followed by that which arrives from Gojjam, and with that of Arsi Nägälle *aräqe* at the rear end. Thus, the notion of trust plays an important role in *aräqe* trade as it does in those of all non-standardized products. People generally tend to attribute high quality to the *aräqe* the origins and makers of which they actually or virtually know, and vice-versa.

5.1.2 Local and Long-Distance Trade

The study has traced the shipment of *aräqe* that is produced in one locality to both close by as well as distant markets, in stages. Firstly, wholesale traders, as a rule, operate by purchasing *aräqe* from distance towns and bringing to

---

[17] Surprisingly enough, this same method of testing homebrewed liquor is also used in other countries, and also goes by the name 'beads' as in Ethiopia where it is commonly known as *č'elle* (ቼሌ).

wholesale in their own hometowns, and never the other way round. They always act as "exporters" in towns which they regularly come to expressly for the business, and act as "importers" in their hometowns.

Secondly, wholesale traders collect the *aräqe* they take away with them directly from distillers at open markets (usually on market days), pouring their various purchases into large 25, 40, or 80 liter jerry cans. In this, they are helped out by tasters as well as brokers/porters to whom they make fixed-rate payments.

Thirdly, wholesale *aräqe* traders ferry away their purchases on open Isuzu or similar trucks which they contract in groups, or with public transport working regular routes. This means that, while wholesale distant traders using contracted trucks reach their destinations in a single stretch, those using public transport could be required to make their trip in more than one stage. For instance, those that operate on the Arsi Nägälle-Dubär route using public transport are forced to break their journey at Addis Ababa in order to switch buses. Those long distance routes with large volume of trade are served with contract trucks while traders working on the less popular routes have to make do with public transport. At Arsi Nägälle, possibly the largest *aräqe* production center in the country, Isuzu trucks dedicated to transporting *aräqe* to particular destinations are found in good number. One, Isuzu truck driver, for instance, has told the researchers that he only works on the Arsi Nägälle-Yabello/Moyale route and he carries only *aräqe*, and that is the only thing he does. At Däbrä Bïrhan, we encountered a group of female *aräqe* traders who were engaged in supplying the towns of Č'äffe and Arb Gäbäya, in Č'äffe Donsa *Wäräda*, with Däbrä Bïrhan *aräqe*. Interestingly enough, on closer examination, we also learnt that one of these ladies was, in fact, the owner-operator of the Isuzu truck. Writing on alcohol in southern Ethiopia, Jon Abbink maintains that the highest priced *aräqe* among the rural people of Maji are those brought "from the Gojjam region or from the Däbrä Bïrhan area" (1997, 13).

Fourthly, it is noteworthy that even most of the long-distance *aräqe* trade is in the hands of women. It is women traders that work the routes between Däbrä Bïrhan, Arsi Nägälle, Dämbäč'a , and Č'anč'o and the many destination towns; and only in one single case – namely, on the Arsi Nägälle-Dubär route – did the study find male businessmen being involved in the trade. Interestingly enough, this particular route is one in which the trader using public transport is required to break his trip passing the night in Addis Ababa, which is inconvenient for women.

Fifth, on arrival at their destination town or market place, wholesale distance traders set up store in market places (usually on market days) under makeshift shades. They often mount their large jerry cans on wooden beds from which they siphon smaller amounts (10 to 20 liters) of *aräqe* into the smaller plastic jerry cans of their customers who will retail it at their homes that are often located in the surrounding rural areas and in some cases even retailers that reside in the urban centers themselves.

The study has identified four major routes followed by the distance and local wholesale *aräqe* trade that is carried on from or in the study areas. The four major routes are: (a) from Däbrä Bïrhan to Č'äffe Donsa, Arb Gäbäya, Sämbo, Šäno, Aleltu, Sändafa, and Addis Ababa, (b) from Arsi Nägälle to Addis Ababa, Dubär, Gorfo, Gurage, Yabello, Moyale, and Gambella, and (c) from Dämbäč'a to Däbrä Marqos, Dubär, Gorfo, and Addis Ababa. Table 7 indicates the direction of the long distance and local wholesale trade in which the study areas are involved.

Table 7. Long distance and local *aräqe* trade routes from or in the study areas

Original Source	Collection Center	Distribution Center	Final Destination (Consumption Target)
Däbrä Bïrhan Town	Däbrä Bïrhan Town	Č'äffe, Arb Gäbäya, Sämbo, Šäno, Aleltu, Sändafa, Addis, etc.	These same towns and their rural hinterlands
Däbrä Bïrhan Town	—	—	Däbrä Bïrhan Town
Rural areas of Bassona Wärana *Wäräda*	Däbrä Bïrhan Town	Č'äffe, Arb Gäbäya, Sämbo, Šäno, Aleltu, Sändafa, Addis, etc.	These same towns and their rural hinterlands
Arsi Nägälle	Arsi Nägälle Town	Gorfo and Dubär	These same towns and their rural hinterlands
		Addis Ababa	Other towns and rural areas
		Moyale, Yabello, Arba Mïnch, Gambella, etc.	These same towns and their rural hinterlands
Rural areas of Dämbäč'a	—	—	Rural areas of Dämbäč'a
Rural areas of Dämbäč'a and Dämbäč'a Town	Dämbäč'a Town	Amanuel, Däbrä Marqos	These same towns and their rural hinterlands
			Other towns and rural areas

Table 7. Cont'd.

Original Source	Collection Center	Distribution Center	Final Destination (Consumption Target)
Č'anč'o Town	Č'anč'o Town	Gorfo and Dubär	Gorfo and Dubär Towns and their rural hinterlands
Rural Čäha	⸺	⸺	Rural Čäha
Urban Čäha	—	—	Urban Čäha

Arsi Nägälle is, of course, a town that is exceptional when it comes not just to the production of *aräqe* but also its marketing. Firstly, although the name Arsi Nägälle has become synonymous with it, *aräqe* is produced not for the town's own consumption, but almost wholly for "export" to other parts of the country. Secondly, this "export trade" even bypasses its immediate hinterland that is generally inhabited by Muslims, targeting far away destinations. Arsi Nägälle's *aräqe* trafficking has spread so wide that the town is now credited with the supply of the whole of southern, southwestern, and central Ethiopia. According to informants from the town, places as distant as the border town of Moyale and remote Gambella fall within the parameter of this trade.

As much as Arsi Nägälle is exceptional for its purely export-oriented production of *aräqe*, Čäha stands out for being devoid of imports and exports of *aräqe*, and its self-sufficiency. Yet, this is not a common feature of even the other *Wärädas* of Gurage Zone. For instance, *aräqe* is imported to the neighboring Gumär *Wäräda* from Hossana.

No specialized "middle-men" who solely engage in the trade of distributing *aräqe* were found operating in any of the study sites; for that reason, the in-depth interview guide that was addressed to such intermediary traders was never used. *Aräqe* is normally distributed to retailers by those same traders who bring it from other places. Only under special circumstances do retailers buy *aräqe* from persons other than those who bring it from other places, since it does not make sense in terms of business. For instance, it is possible for a retailer who happens to run out of her home brewed or "imported" supply to borrow or even buy *aräqe* at a loss in order not to turn away some regular and valued clients.

Likewise, the study did not find evidence in support of the existence of relay long-distance trade in *aräqe*. Long-distance traders operate directly between the place of origin, where the *aräqe* is distilled, and its final destination.

Plate 5: *Aräqe* peddling and collection

Top: Roadside *Aräqe* peddlers along the Dämbäč'a – Bahir Dar highway

Bottom: A collection wholesale traders in action, Däbrä Bïrhan Market

Plate 6: Aräqe market and wholesalers manning their collection stalls

Top: A group of women wholesalers ready to get their purchases loaded. Däbrä Bïrhan Market

Bottom: A professional *aräqé* taster in action. Arsi Nägälle Market

Plate 7: Wholesalers distributing *Aräqe* in their hometowns

Top: A wholesaler siphoning *aräqe* into the bottle of a retailer at his stall in Dubär market

Bottom: Another wholesaler siphoning *aräqé* into a smaller jerry can of a retailer by the sidewalk of the main highway in Dubär Town

5.1.3 Marketing of Ingredients and Implements, and Delivery of Related Services

The marketing of *aräqe* production ingredients and implements is as important as that of the *aräqe* itself. Trade in *aräqe* grains, malt, *gešo*, aromatic woods, and firewood, as well as production and marketing apparatus such as clay jars, bamboo pipes, clay bawls, clay head-cup, plastic jars, jerry cans, and plastic water bottles play a significant role in the economy of the urban and rural areas where *aräqe* is produced.

Although we were unable to quantify the magnitude of the trade in *aräqe* ingredients and implements in the various study sites, their importance is highlighted by the situation in the most developed *aräqe* production and marketing center, namely, Arsi Nägälle. Here, the economy of scale in *aräqe* production has obviously induced a commensurate growth in the magnitude of the trade in *aräqe* ingredients. This is indicated, among others, by the emergence of one or more specialized marketplaces for each of the major ingredients, namely, *aräqe* grains, malt, *gešo*, aromatic woods, and firewood.

Even in the rest of the study sites, there appears to be a trend in the growing importance of the trade in *aräqe* ingredients and implements. For instance, in the town of Dubär, a trader has specialized in the importation of the potent but toxic grain of *ïnkïrdad* to the town.

The importance of *aräqe*-related services such as flour milling and transportation of ingredients, and the likes cannot be overstated. Although this is true of all production and/or marketing centers, it is better exemplified by taking, once again, the more developed case of Arsi Nägälle as an example.

5.2 Retail Trade

Aräqe is retailed in one of two ways, by the same establishment that acts act as both on-premise and off-premise outlet. It is either sold by the bottle for off-premise consumption or served on-premise by the shot glass. In the first case people buy *aräqe* by the bottle which they carry away with them. They avail themselves of this kind of purchase during individual or group visits to families that are in mourning or in celebration, or on occasions such as after mediations or business deals, when the main protagonists have to entertain all those in attendance with rounds of *aräqe* symbolically "sealing" the deal. The second, i.e., on-premise service by the shot glass, is the most important type of retailing both in terms of volume and impact, and for which reason it is discussed following its various types, as retailing that takes place in: (1) specialized *aräqe*-tavern and mainly *aräqe*-tavern, (2) drinking establishment and/or eateries that also retail *aräqe*, and (3) ordinary homes that now and then double as *aräqe*-tavern.

5.2.1 Specialized Aräqe Tavern and Mainly Aräqe Tavern

Specialized *aräqe* taverns (*aräqe bets*) and establishments the main business of which is serving *aräqe* by the shot glass are urban and village center phenomena. Few, if any, are found in rural areas. Their arrival at village centers is a recent development that has followed the steady growth in the disposable income of farmers, and the proliferation of sizable village centers thanks to, among other things, the movement of a large number of government employees (extension workers and teachers in particular) to rural villages, and the recent electrification of most of them.

Specialized *aräqe* taverns are places where the *aräqe* that is sold there is also produced there. They are also places of residence where the single or married women that produce and serve the *aräqe* live together with their families, since these people cannot afford to maintain separate living quarters and to stay away from the location of their business for any length of time. As a result, although some have pet names, they normally do not carry official names or display proper signposts, or put up tell-tale signs such as the tin-can mounted pegs in front of *t'älla* taverns, the false-banana leaves that hang by the entrance of *č'at bets*, and the eucalyptus branches that mark *ïnjära bets*[18]. Yet, since these are places where *aräqe* is served to the public on a regular basis, they qualify as taverns.

It was also learnt that some of these *aräqe* taverns, in addition to now and then providing treats, engage on the side in the sale of soft drinks, tea, and bread. Soft drinks are made available for the benefit of non-alcohol drinking guests that come with regular *aräqe* tavern customers. Tea and bread are served by some *aräqe* taverns, as in Dämbäč'a town, until midday and mainly to students — a practice that has sprung to life following the recent increase in the number of children attending school.

---

[18] It is noteworthy, that all traditional fermented and distilled alcoholic drinks in Ethiopia are never advertised through posters, and the mass media such as television, radio, and newspaper commercials. The single exception to this is the case of a factory produced brand of *t'äj* by the name of SABA TEJ that briefly saw the light of day back in the 1960s, which is understandable considering the fact that it had to operate by the marketing principles of the modern industrial sector to which it belonged. (NB: This earlier factory production of *t'äj* in Ethiopia should not to be confused with a similar product that is currently being manufactured and marketed in the US under the same brand name – www.heritagewines.com).

Clients are served and entertained by "professional" waitresses only in exceptional types of urban *aräqe* taverns – exceptional in that they are located in the red-light districts of the towns and the waitresses are professional sex-workers. In all other types of *aräqe* taverns and retail outlets, *aräqe* is served by the female head of the household and/or by her helpers, who could be her sisters, daughters, or other relatives.

The *aräqe* taverns in the study areas differ widely in size as well as standards in terms of space, building and furniture quality, as well as neatness and hygiene. In general, both the size and standards of the *aräqe* taverns are positively correlated with the level of urbanity and size of the urban center in which they are located. Thus, by far the largest and most "classy" of them all, popularly known as *Adaraš* (the Hall) are found in Däbrä Bïrhan (see Plate 8). The majority of those in Dubär, Ïmdïbïr, and Dämbäč'a are middle-level, while most of those in Gorfo and Qäyït are smaller and of lower standards. Although *aräqe* taverns of the different sizes and standards are typical of the different sized towns, all of the town's house *aräqe* taverns of lower standards that are usually run by new immigrant women from the surrounding rural areas and are not in many regards much different from the rural homes in which *aräqe* is occasionally retailed (see Plate 9). Even the *aräqe* that is served in such taverns is often of inferior quality, such as the type popularly known by the derogatory term "*kolombia*", or Arsi Nägälle's poorest quality product known as "*boč'e*" in its place of origin, and Dämbäč'a's third-rater called "*šäratä*".

As opposed to the patrons of *aräqe* retailing rural homes who are all locals and socially homogenous, clients of urban *aräqe* taverns are as varied as the taverns themselves. The classy ones are the choice of the towns' elite – businessmen, government workers and other grandees (or "people who keep up to protocol" in the words of one informant). The middle-level *aräqe* taverns are the kind that many men find to be sufficiently decent while affordable or that many young men are attracted to by the other forms of entertainment including commercial sex. Finally, *aräqe* taverns of lower standards are the favourite hangout of the urban poor and rural visitors who flood the urban marketplaces.

The study has also found out the existence of establishments that in addition to mainly engaging in the sale of take-away food items such as *ïnjära* and fresh meat and serving cooked food and/or other drinks on-premise, also serve *aräqe* as a sort of add-on activity. This is a practice found in the towns of Sululta, where integrated butcheries, small eateries, and drinking places are more common than in the other sites of this study and where *aräqe* is sold as an auxiliary activity only to facilitate that side of the business which is more important to the establishment, i.e., as "a means of warming up the other business" (የቀረውን ንግድ እንደ ማሟሟቂያ), in the words of the informants themselves.

Plate 8: *Aräqe* **taverns of varying standards - I**

Top: Adaraš (the Hall) of Däbrä Bïrhan, the favorite hangout of the town's elite for *aräqe*

Bottom: An ordinary *aräqe* tavern of Gorfo Market Town

Plate 9: *Äräqe* taverns of varying standards - II

Top: An ordinary *äräqe* tavern of Ïmdïbïr Town

Bottom: A low-end *äräqe* tavern frequented by rural visitors of Dämbäč'a Town

5.2.2 Homes That Now and Then Double as Aräqe Tavern

As noted earlier, all *aräqe* taverns serve the additional purpose of residential space to the distiller-retailers and their families. However, there is a special category that is somewhat different from the foregoing in that it consists of *bona fide* – even ancestral – homes where *aräqe* is sold by the shot glass only irregularly. The sociological distinctiveness of this category of *aräqe* outlets can be better appreciated when one realizes that it consists of "establishments": (1) that are rural homes of farming families where the women folk undertake the business of retailing *aräqe* by the shot glass, (2) that are run as a subsidiary and part-time activity by women whose primary occupation is agriculture – commonly referred to as "outdoor work" by the women themselves, (3) the women usually engage only in the retailing of *aräqe* which they themselves have distilled and only in exceptional cases that which they buy from wholesalers, (4) that, due to the relatively small size and low density of population of the rural communities, cater to small circles of clients that are acquainted to the women and to one another, thus giving the business less of a public nature.

This type of *aräqe* retailing, which occurs in all of the study sites, is more common in some than in others. For instance, Čäha is remarkable in that all its *aräqe* distillers retail their product at home by the shot glass and do not sell it to wholesalers or other retailers.

5.2.3 Aräqe Retailing and Sex Work

The paths of *aräqe* retailing and sex do converge, but not necessarily always. Sexual liaison between clients and waitresses of establishments where *aräqe* is retailed by the shot glass occurs only in the context of the "red light" district *aräqe* taverns for which paid sex is the main object of attraction for clients. Here, the role that is played by *aräqe* is the same as that of alcoholic drinks in general: enticement, loss of guard, and surrender to the hired waitress cum sex-worker, more sales of *aräqe* for the tavern owner, and both for an owner who also serves drinks and provides paid sexual service.

Aräqe taverns where waitresses cum sex-workers are employed by owners for the purpose of facilitating the sale of *aräqe* are common in the "red light" district of Central Däbrä Bïrhan Town. In the smaller towns of Č'anč'o, Qäyït, and Dubär, on the other hand, a few owner-waitresses that also engage in paid sex are found, although their number has declined since the advent of HIV and AIDS.

In addition to the above, there is a strange practice of renting beds, mattresses, and earthen sleeping beds in which *aräqe* taverns engaged, although this has reportedly waned to the point of becoming extinct under the double pressures of HIV/AIDS and the awareness created about it. Under this practice, couples maintaining illicit sexual liaison would enter an *aräqe* tavern on the pretext of having drinks and proceed to make use of the bedding facility it provided.

5.3 Significance of Aräqe Marketing

The significance of *aräqe* marketing can be looked at two distinct, albeit interrelated levels, namely, that of the individual and the community.

5.3.1 Significance for the Individual

Aräqe marketing is significant primarily for those individuals that engage in it as a major source of income. Both wholesalers and retailers derive substantial incomes from marketing *aräqe* as compared to those who only distil it and pass it to others to sell.

A wholesale trader in *aräqe* who purchases his commodity in Arsi Nägälle and ferries it all the way to Dubär in Sululta *Wäräda*, makes a net profit of 18-20 Birr per 60-liter jerry can, or 30-33 cents per liter of *aräqe*. Since each of these wholesalers "import" 4-6 jerry cans of *aräqe* per trip, on average, they would make some 72-120 Birr for every 3-day trip they make plus some 1-2 days that it takes to clear their purchases.

The money earned by selling *aräqe* by the shot is even more substantial. For instance, in rural Dämbäč'a, a 750 ml bottle of *aräqe* the wholesale price of which is 9 Birr, would retail for 18 Birr. In Däbrä Bïrhan, distillers deliver to wholesalers or retailers a liter of *aräqe* for 16 Birr, but retail it themselves by the shot glass for 20 Birr – on average. However, further deductions are in this case in order as retailers by the shot glass incur costs of housing, furniture, utensils, and utilities.

Assuming the cost of labor is equal across wholesale and retail marketing, it is obvious from the above presentation that retailing *aräqe* appears to be much more lucrative. This is so per unit of measure – some 4-9 Birr profit per liter of *aräqe* retailed by the shot glass in Dämbäč'a and Däbrä Bïrhan versus 30-33 Cents per liter for *aräqe* that is brought from Arsi Nägälle and wholesale marketed in Sululta. However, since wholesalers deal in larger volumes than retailers theirs is more favored by the advantage of economy of scale.

Considering the above, then, it is not at all surprising that most *aräqe* distillers also engage in marketing their product, and still some more women prefer to engage only in the retailing end of the *aräqe* business.

Aräqe retailing has an additional function that further contributes to its significance, namely its function to assist in the sale of other commodities that are central to the line of business in which a certain establishment is primarily engaged. Informants who engage in retailing *aräqe* only as an "add-on" activity said they indulge in it only as a means of boosting or "warming up" (ማግማጊቷይ) their main business that consists of serving food or selling take-away *ïnjära* or fresh meat.

5.3.2 Significance for the Community at Large

The significance of *aräqe* marketing — both wholesale and retail — for the communities at large cannot be overstated. It is, for instance, hard to imagine their markets, the service sector of their economy, urban development including housing, and in some cases even municipal revenue without the buying and selling of *aräqe* which also contributes to most other businesses.

Yet, there are marked differences between the various sites of the study as regards this. *Aräqe* marketing definitely holds a central place in the economic and social life of Arsi Nägälle, followed by Däbrä Bïrhan, Dubär, Gorfo, Qäyït, Dämbäč'a town, and Ïmdïbïr in that order while it is generally of a lesser significance in the rural areas. Moreover, there are differences among the various sites regarding which type of *aräqe* marketing is more important to them: wholesale, retail, or both?

In none of the study sites was *aräqe* marketing as important as in Arsi Nägälle. By extension, there is no urban center in the country, including Addis Ababa, in which *aräqe* marketing is as prominent as in Arsi Nägälle. According to an official in the town administration, there is very little in the town that has nothing to do with *aräqe*: (1) *aräqe* production and marketing accounts for 85% of all employment in this town, which is incidentally middle-sized by Ethiopian standards with a population of 62,058 in 2007; (2) it is the driving force behind the 50 flour-milling establishments, each of which has an average of 5 mills; (3) a large fleet of horse carts numbering 560 and innumerable crude wheelbarrows ferrying around either *aräqe*, its ingredients, or people engaged in its production and/or marketing; and (4) *aräqe* is a sizable source of municipal revenue that has gone up from an average of 22,000 Birr per week in 2007/8 to an average of 25,000 Birr per week in September 2009, and again to 31,000 in December 2009 that is obtained from taxing *aräqe* that leaves the town at the rate of 0.05 Birr per liter; (5) given that 620,000 liters of *aräqe* was being exported per week at the end of 2009, this gives an annual export volume of 32,240,000 liters. On the other hand, the second important *aräqe* center, Däbrä Bïrhan, exported 75,000 liters of *aräqe* per week in September 2009, which adds up to 3,900,000 liters per annum (one-eighth that of Arsi Nägälle).

5.4 Impact of Aräqe Marketing

5.4.1 Impact on Retailing Families

The study has found out that *aräqe* marketing has mixed impacts on families and family members that engage in it. Regarding marital relations among couples in whose homes *aräqe* is retailed, we have learnt that the frequency and level of the conflict that crops up between them are not significantly different from those in the general population, excepting those *aräqe* retailing families in which the husband is himself a heavy drinker. Informants were unanimous in their view that in those cases in which the husband is alcohol dependent, marital conflicts and turmoil within the whole family are common since such husbands endlessly demand to be served with free *aräqe*, and pick up fights with family members and even with clients. Thus, it should be noted that this is as much, if not more, a problem of *aräqe* consumption as it is that of its marketing. In *aräqe* retailing families in which husbands are free of alcohol dependence, on the other hand, informants — including married women who retail *aräqe* — maintain that, normally, all members share the workload thus demonstrating a strong sense of family solidarity.

The study's inquiry regarding the welfare of children in *aräqe* retailing families, which has included in-depth interviews with such children, has produced mixed results. On the one hand, we have learnt of cases in which children that were raised in homes in which *aräqe* was being regularly retailed, i.e., *aräqe* taverns, went on to be well educated and successful later in life. Informants generally agreed that these children are not in any way less well behaved as compared to children in the general population. As regards, the educational performance of these children, however, some informants — particularly teachers – held the view that they perform below standard due to the fact that the various chores with which they are encumbered prevent them from undertaking their homework and from going to bed early.

Box 4: The Case of Wäyzäro Kälämäwärq

> Wäyzäro Kälämäwärq Ahmäd was born and raised in Wällo, which she left in her teens some 30 years-ago to come and live in Gorfo, Sululta Wäräda, with her cousin who worked for the Ethiopian Highway Authority,. She got used to the new place so much that she remained behind even when her cousin left together with the Highway work camp.
>
> Wäyzäro Kälämäwärkq settled down, got married, and bore children in her adopted homeland. For want of anything better to do with her spare time, and in order to help in the family's relentless struggle to make ends meet, she got started in *aräqe*-making business which she had learnt during her days in Wällo.
>
> As time passed, however, her husband could not find gainful employment anywhere in the Sululta Wäräda area, and settled for a life of an itinerant casual worker that kept him away from home for several days and weeks at a time. This was an arrangement that was doomed not to last, and so, considering the "danger of the times" that was lurking, she divorced her husband some 10 years ago.
>
> Wäyzäro Kälämäwärq has added a couple of children since her divorce, and the family has been subsisting only on income she derives from the making and retailing of *aräqe* in her tiny two-room house and the messy kitchen attached to it. But, after all is said and done, Wäyzäro Kelemework has not just managed to survive, but has fared quite well. She has succeeded in keeping her children going to school, and one of her daughters has graduated from high school and has landed a job with the Sululta *Wäräda* Administration. Wäyzäro Kelemework is a proud mother, and her children happy. Not surprisingly, they always declare that none of this would have been possible without her *aräqe* business.

5.4.2 Impact on the Local Community

The impact of *aräqe* retailing on the local community at large differs from place to place. In Däbrä Bïrhan and Qäyït, *aräqe* taverns, informants maintained, are the dens for sex-workers and criminals. They say some of these taverns are the bases where criminals meet, hatch and launch their next operation from, and retreat to afterwards. They are epicenters of public disturbances, noise pollution, and various sorts of illegal transactions; or were so until the very recent reduction in the level of crime following the introduction of the 'community policing program' in the Zone. The popular name by which the red-light district of *Qäbäle* 02 in Däbrä Bïrhan that houses most of the *aräqe* taverns in the town is known, Katanga, says it all.

With the support of his fellow discussants, one member of the elders' FGD in Qäyït characterized the *aräqe bets* in that market town, particularly those of *Tägulät Säfär*, as follows:

> Some of the *aräqe bets*, particularly those of *Tägulät Säfär*, are the dens of criminals, including hired hands. Criminal deeds are hatched and deals made there. They also serve criminals as safe houses where they lay in wait reinforcing their resolve with rounds of *aräqe*, launch their attacks from, and withdraw to as their first point of retreat once their evil deeds are done.

In the rest of the study sites – Sululta, Dämbäč'a, Čäha, and Arsi Nägälle – on the other hand, *aräqe* retailing by itself is not associated with crime and public disturbances. According to informants, the fights and disturbances that take place here are said to occur outside of the taverns and in open public places such as marketplaces, public transport terminals, roads and open spaces including those outside church closures. In other words, *aräqe* retailing is not directly responsible for the fights and disturbances in that they take place separate from the process of retailing, but indirectly since they are the sources of the *aräqe* that is consumed, intoxicates, and drives people to such acts.

VI. Aräqe Consumption

In the same way that the divisibility, long shelf-life, portability, and high unit value of *aräqe* made it a commodity of significance throughout most of the Ethiopian highlands[19], so also, its crystal clear appearance, stinging taste, supposed digestive and medicinal qualities, as well as its relative affordability as compared to factory produced beverages, have conspired to make *aräqe* the drink of choice for a multitude of Ethiopians. In spite of its ills to individual, communities, and society at large that is well recognized by its consumers, its popularity and overall level of consumption has grown to the extent that there remains only few pockets of the population and corners of the country that still remain beyond its clutches.

The subsections that follow present the findings of the study as regards consumption levels, trends, consuming cohorts, and drinking patterns and norms as well as impacts of *aräqe* consumption.

6.1 Current Patterns and Emerging Trends in *Aräqe* Consumption

6.1.1 Overall Consumption Levels and General Trends

The questions regarding current levels of *aräqe* consumption and whether *aräqe* consumption has increased, decreased, or remained the same ever since its introduction can be adequately pursued if, in addition to being area specific, they are made to refer to two separate albeit interrelated aspects of consumption: (1) proportion of *aräqe* consumers in the adult population, together with (2) their level of consumption/dependency. Although the study was not aimed at and designed to systematically operationalize, quantify, and measure these aspects of *aräqe* consumption, it has obtained the rough estimates of focus groups members consisting of elders, CBO leaders, religious leaders, businesswomen, businessmen, and farmers that were enlisted at four of its sites. (The issue of consumption as a whole was not pursued in the fifth site, Arsi Nägälle, since this site was included in the study only for its role as a major producing area serving far away consumers including those in some of the other study sites).

Table 8 gives the estimated percentage distributions of adult populations obtained from the focus groups at the respective sites, by sex, and consumption status. Being the rough estimates by focus group members, these distributions

---

[19] Historically, liquor had come to be valued so much in some countries that it was temporarily used as a medium of exchange in the same way *amole* served the purpose in the Ethiopian highlands not so long ago. Such, for instance, was the case with rum in New England and New South Wales for a time (Blue 2004, Microsoft Encarta 2009).

ought to be taken as simply as general indicators of the situation as perceived by significant community members, and not as data that are derived through actual measurement. Whereas what the focus groups identified as 'dependent drinker' is quite clearly the equivalent of 'alcoholic', those whom they considered to be 'ordinary drinkers' are all who "drink regularly, but not every day and not beyond their limit".

Table 8. Estimates of current percentage distribution of adult population by site, sex, and *aräqe* consumption status

Study Site	*Aräqe* Consumption Status								
	% Abstainers			% Ordinary Drinkers			% Dependent Drinkers		
	Male	Female	Both	Male	Female	Both	Male	Female	Both
Sululta-Dubär	10	80	45	75	15	45	15	5	10
Qäyït (Bassona Wärana)	10	90	50	70	10	40	20	0	10
Yäšäboč (Dämbäč'a)	5	25	15	80	65	72.5	15	10	12.5
Yäfeq-T'äräq (Čaha)	30	100	65	70	0	35	0	0	0
Average Percentage	13.75	73.75	43.75	73.75	22.5	48.13	12.5	3.75	8.13

By looking at the totals of the estimated percentages of 'ordinary' *aräqe* drinkers and *aräqe* 'dependents' in the four sites, as well as at the 'overall totals', one can appreciate the extent to which *aräqe* consumption has got hold of the society. In all of the four sites, for instance, *aräqe* is consumed by 30% or more of the adult male population, and excepting Yäfeq-T'äräq of Čaha, it is consumed by 90-95 percent of male adults. What is more worrying is the level of *aräqe* dependency that emerges from Table 8. Fifteen to 20 percent of the male populations of Däbrä Bïrhan-Qäyït, Sululta-Dubär, and Dämbäč'a-Yäšäboč were estimated to be *aräqe* dependent.

Aräqe consumption is on the rise more-or-less everywhere. Having looked into the interrelated issues of change in the number of *aräqe* consumers and change in level of consumption per person as well as the direction of the changes, the study has revealed rising trends in both cases. In all of the study sites, individual informants and focus group participants were unanimous in their opinion that the number of people that consume *aräqe* as well as the level at which they consume it has been increasing significantly in their respective localities. As one informant from Dämbäč'a noted, "from government to government, both living conditions and *aräqe* [consumption] have improved"

(ከመንግሥት መንግሥት ፤ ኑሮም አረቄም አብረው ተሻሽለዋል). Moreover, even when informants made mention of signs of a slight reversal in the growing trend in *aräqe* consumption in very recent years, as they did in Čäha, it was in connection with some countermeasures that were taken by religious and indigenous institutions, primarily because things were getting out of hand and something had to be done about it at the local level. (For the comparative position of the Sub-Saharan Africa region regarding alcohol consumption, see Annex 6).

6.1.2 Consuming Cohorts and New Trends in Consumer Groups

Men are by far the main consumers of *aräqe*. The previous table, Table 8, shows the existence of marked differences between males and females in *aräqe* consumption in the four sites of the study. This is not at all surprising considering the fact that the drinking or over-drinking of liquor by women is culturally discouraged everywhere, and considered a taboo in the case of Čäha. Yet, the fact that 75, 20, and 10 percent of the women in Yäšäboč of Dämbäč'a, Dubär of Sululta, and Qäyït of Bassona Wärana *Wäräda, respectively*, were estimated to be drinkers, and particularly that 10 and 5 percent of the women in the first two sites were deemed to be *aräqe* dependents by the focus groups is indicative of the existence of an alarming situation even as regards women.

Aräqe is consumed much more by middle-aged and older men as compared to youngsters. Informants in all of the study sites save Dämbäč'a maintained that the young in their respective localities demonstrate clear preference for *t'äj* and beer and in some cases for *č'at*, at the expense of *aräqe*. This, however, is not to say that there are no young people that are habituated to drinking *aräqe* or that *aräqe* drinking has stopped at the age cohort that is presently young. In fact, the normal trajectory is for a young age cohort to graduate to *aräqe* drinking as it grows older.

Dämbäč'a *Wäräda* is altogether dissimilar from the other study sites when it comes to *aräqe* consumption by the young. According to our informants, although the amount of *aräqe* young men in Dämbäč'a consume is not comparable to that of their elders', they get introduced to *aräqe* drinking from the tender age of seven and continue with it throughout their lives.

There is also some dissimilarity between rural people and urbanites as regards *aräqe* consumption. A larger proportion of the rural population regularly drinks *aräqe* as compared to that of the urban population that has better access to factory-made alcoholic beverages, namely, the various types of liquor (*yä färänj aräqe*) and beer. Some urbanites totally avoid *aräqe*, preferring the factory-processed beverages, while others drink lesser amounts of *aräqe* as they can make up for the difference by drinking the factory products.

Contrary to common sense expectation that a significant proportion of *aräqe* drinkers would switch to factory-made alcoholic beverages to the same extent as the improvement in their cash income, the share of *aräqe* drinkers in the population has not gone down. Oddly enough, it has gone up; and one informant explained this seemingly bizarre state of affairs by saying, "As our cash income has increased lately, we have become more and more capable of accessing *aräqe*, but since the prices of the factory made alcoholic beverages have also sky-rocketed during the same time, they have remained beyond our reach."

Informants also cited the relatively marked potency of the indigenous *aräqe* as one more advantage it has over factory-made alcoholic beverages, making it the drink of choice for people with limited financial resources.

6.1.3 Patterns of Consumption

One other area of interest of this study has been the ways and means under which *aräqe* is consumed by the people of the study areas. This refers to *the occasions* during which, *where*, *when*, and together *with what food items* it is consumed.

The main occasions during which people in the study sites generally drink *aräqe* are: visits to weekly markets, weddings, baptisms (*kïrïstïna*), mediations (*ïrq*), sale of significant assets (*yä fünt'ïr*), congratulatory gatherings on different pretexts (*yä däsdäs*), post-funeral stopovers at *aräqe* taverns, visits to mourning houses where *aräqe* is brought by individuals or groups (*yä ïzïn*), and memorial services held at the house of deceased persons (*täzkar, yä arba dïgïs*), among others. All of these occasions are social in that they relate to community or group affairs. Considering the number and variety of these social occasions, one can easily understand the impossibility for people of these communities to escape the web of drinking circles and drinking opportunities.

Traditionally, participants at reciprocal labor-pooling work events (*jïgi/däbo*) are fed with bread (*dabo*) and local beer (*t'älla*), and at most with *ïnjära* and *wät'*. Yet, *aräqe* has penetrated even this unlikely occasion where people would be expected to do expend their energy on the work at hand. Such is the situation in Sululta and Čäha, and in the latter case even casual workers do not start the day's work unless their employer supplies them from the outset with some *aräqe* by way of bonus.

On the contrary, *aräqe* is not consumed at church-based group festivities (*sänbätes*), according to most of our informants. However, other informants and focus group discussants maintained that the issue of whether *aräqe* should be served on these occasions and particularly at memorial church services for the dead (*qurban*) following which food and the local beer (*t'älla*) are normally the drinks provided to the priesthood and the needy has remained contentious.

Although the matter is not yet solved for the Church as a whole, many parish churches have banned *aräqe* at least from inner church premises since a year or so ago.

Under normal circumstances, *aräqe* is always consumed within closed space. The main places of consumption are, of course, the retailing outlets of various types where *aräqe* is sold by the shot glass to be consumed on-premise (alongside sale for off-premise consumption). In addition to these, then, there are other arenas where *aräqe* is consumed particularly in connection with social occasions mentioned earlier. Since these occasions naturally involve social gatherings, the *aräqe* consumption that takes place in this case does so in social arenas. These include not just *bona fide* public places such as the inner church premises (*däje sälam*), the outer church grounds (*margäja*), market places, and places of religious and cultural festivities such as riverside spots where Epiphany is celebrated. Even private spaces such as those homes in which people are sitting in mourning as well as homes in which weddings and similar celebrations are being held can be considered temporarily public, since they acquire some of the features of public places for the duration of the events.

As for the time of day, days of the week, and seasons during which *aräqe* is normally consumed (although the most important variations are individual as those that are *aräqe* dependent consume it at all times), there are some differences between the study sites. (1) Firstly, drinking of *aräqe* before noon is proscribed and not practiced in rural Čäha; in Sululta some people resort to it despite its being discouraged; in Däbrä Bïrhan there are many who do so as it is not discouraged except for fasting days; in rural Dämbäč'a, drinking *aräqe* as a morning pick-me-up is preferred and widely practiced. (2) Secondly, the practice of drinking *aräqe* from early afternoon onwards (and on fasting days from mid-afternoon onwards) is considered normal everywhere, and all of our informants were of the opinion that they see nothing inappropriate in doing this as they themselves indulge in it. (3) Thirdly, in all of the study sites, more *aräqe* is consumed on market days, weekends, and patron-saints' days than on ordinary days. In particular, the consumption of *aräqe* on market days by the multitude of rural people who visit the towns is excessive because of the opportunity for anonymity offered to them by the towns and the loosening of social controls thereof. (4) There is no seasonal variation in the level of consumption of *aräqe*, save for fasting seasons, in any of the study sites.

Although drinking after having a bite or two is preferred, if and when such food is available (**ከተገኘ፤ ትንሽ ምናምን አፍ ላይ ማድረግ**), drinking *aräqe* on an empty stomach is quite common in all the study sites. As for types of food that are commonly consumed before or after drinking *aräqe*, only in rural Dämbäč'a did informants repeatedly tell of the practice of being served with and eating plain *ïnjära* (i.e., without hot red pepper sauce (*wät'*), in order not to add another burning factor into the equation) right before the drinking of *aräqe* begins. Other than this, no convention regarding what one should eat before or after drinking *aräqe* was found operating in any of the study sites.

The only standardized and universally established practice of *aräqe* drinking relates to the serving small glassware and chinaware. The 50-milliliter shot glass (*mäläkia*) is the one with which *aräqe* is universally retailed, obviously because amounts that are sold have to be measured in terms of counts of a standard sized glass with a known price (see Box 5 for its early introduction). The small, handleless, china coffee-cup (*yä bunna sïni*) is what is commonly used for drinking *aräqe* in peoples' homes, where glassware is in short supply and the coffee-cup that is a fixture of practically every Ethiopian home also serves very well as a standard unit of measurement.

Box 5: Menelik, His Greek Merchant, and the Small Serving Glass

> As the story goes, Emperor Menelik, having given a certain Greek merchant the sole right to import various types of liquor such as the Metaxa cognac for the first time ever, soon learnt that many of his courtiers and other big men were getting in the habit of taking a glass too many of the new arrival and as a result getting over-intoxicated to the point of making fools of themselves. He was told of, for instance, how certain high ranking officials became the laughingstock of the public when they repeatedly failed to pass the unavoidable test of mounting their mules, and so on. Upon hearing all this, the Emperor summoned the Greek merchant whom he proceeded to half-angrily and half-jokingly castigate for turning his men into drunkards. To this, the Greek is said to respond as follows: Yes Sire, it is true that I have imported these highly potent and seductive drinks. But, it is also true that I had brought along with the stuff, a tiny glass with which to drink it in small measures. It is your men who threw away the small glass and resorting to the use of their *t'äj* drinking "Menelik Cup" that are to blame, not me who brought something new together with its appropriate scale!

6.1.4 Spread of Aräqe Consumption and Community Norms

What emerges from the foregoing discussions is the dearth of conventions, norms, and taboos that restrict or regulate how, under which occasions, in which places, by whom, at what times, and with what food intake *aräqe* should or should not be consumed. Other than the use of a standard shot glass in retailing *aräqe*, there are very few practices that are governed by socially embedded rules with which *aräqe* consumption is regulated. In those cases in which some norms exist, they seem to be local in the making, and incomplete. For instance, while there are some community norms against drunkenness in public places, there are no rules against the drinking of *aräqe* itself. In fact, even drunkenness is excused or is used as an excuse for unacceptable behavior. People are often heard saying "I need to drink because of this and that reason" and also apologizing for others by saying "He did this and that because/while he was drunk".

What has been learnt through this study regarding this lacuna and also about the recent nature of the introduction and spread of *aräqe* consumption in the study areas, taken together, are capable of providing us with sufficient ground to make the following important proposition. *A chemically potent and socially disruptive substance abuse has run out of control and is progressively taking hold of the society leading it into uncharted lanes with potentially serious negative consequences (see Box 6). This situation is the result of the rapid introduction and spread of aräqe consumption in rural and small-town Ethiopia, on the one hand, and the lag in the emergence of community norms governing it, on the other.*

Box 6: The Consequence of Sudden Change in Drinking Habits

In the course of the exploratory queries that were undertaken in 1992, the first author of this work had the privilege of discussing *aräqe* issues with a knowledgeable gentleman by the name of Ato Bogalä Abäbä, who, while a long-time resident of Addis Ababa, had maintained strong links with Č'äfe Donsa where he was born and raised. The late Ato Bogalä, who was already in his 80s at the time of the interview, communicated to this author his observation on the issue as well as a number of enlightening anecdotes, including the following.

One day in the 1950s, I and two of my friends went to Č'äfe Donsa for the burial of a mutual acquaintance of ours. After the burial ceremony was over, we were served lavishly with food and drinks in the church yard which we consumed with the kind of enthusiasm that only hungry men can harbor. As we had to get back to Addis Ababa before night fall and since we had to do quite a bit of walking to the Addis Ababa – Asmara road to get public transport, we left the church as early as we could and started to rush towards Addis.

Somewhere in between, however, we were stopped by a rich farmer that was a childhood friend of all three of us. The man implored us to enter his house and partake of the meal he had prepared for us, having expressly slaughtered a sheep for the sole purpose of our visit. We tried to explain to him that we were already full to our brim with food which we had eaten at the church, not knowing that he was preparing a feast for us. After a lengthy negotiation, the matter was settled with a compromise according to which we would go into his house "in order to just taste the food and drinks". That was what actually followed. We could only taste them and leave.

Unfortunately, another local gentleman who was apparently given to observing and interpreting things was also present in our host's place, and on one of the following days, this person explained to our host the reason for our failure to consume more of the food and drinks that were served. He said to him pointedly that we left briskly without as much as touching any of the food and drinks because of their inferior quality and the standards to which we "city folks" were accustomed. He also advised our host that he should promptly deal with the situation by taking a new wife and getting his domestic life in order.

Within a few short months our host who was a member of the landed local gentry divorced the mother of his children, gave her a large piece of land and animals enough for a comfortable retirement, and got himself a new wife from the lowlands to the east. The new wife who was selected mainly for her culinary skills brought to her new domicile a variety of cuisines and a generous consumption regime. The rather gentler and healthier sauces of old gave way to strong and spiced ones, milk and *qïrare* were replaced with *t'älla* and most of all *aräqe*, but sadly enough, the latter strong beverages continued to be served with the same cups and frequency as the former ones.

The next time I came to Č'äfe Donsa and visited my old friend, I found him blind and bedridden. The unregulated consumption of *aräqe* by an unaware and unsuspecting person who is newly introduced to it has caused an irreparable harm. I always remember the incident that triggered it all and regret it to this day.

6.2 Impacts of Aräqe Consumption

It has long been established that alcohol abuse has harmful physical, mental, and social consequences. The most serious of all of these is probably alcohol-related mortality and morbidity. A WHO expert committee estimated that alcohol causes a net harm of 3.7% of all deaths, and 4.4% of the global burden of disease (2007). Furthermore, studies have shown that alcohol-related illnesses and diseases can be acute or short-term and those developed over the long term (See Annex 5 for details)

The acute harms of alcohol include inflammation of the gut lining, inflammation of the pancreas, heart arrhythmias, high blood pressure, shortness of breath, cardiac failure, stroke, and gastro-oesophageal haemorrhage as well as road injuries, fall injuries, fire injuries, drowning, and occupational and machine injuries and assault. On the other hand, the health consequences of chronic alcohol abuse include several types of cancer, liver cirrhosis (scarring of the liver), mental problems, heart problems, and sexual problems (Parliament of Victoria Drugs and Crime Prevention Committee 2004; WHO 2007; WHO 2000).

It is also worth mentioning the strong link between alcohol and HIV. Amoateng, Acheampong, Kalule-Sabiti, and Narayanan (2007) cite several studies that have found alcohol and drug use can increase the risk of infection with such sexually transmitted diseases. Similarly, a study comissioned by the U.S. Agency for International Development verified that 'alcohol influences high risk behavior, such as unprotected casual and indiscriminate sex, sex with commercial sex workers and unprotected sex with multiple partners' which are likely to lead to infection with HIV (cited in Morris *et al.* 2006).

The impact of alcohol, however, goes much beyond the illnesses/accidents experienced by alcohol abusers and includes those felt by the community as a whole. Alcohol-related crime and violence fall in this category. The fact that alcohol contributes to the commission of crimes such as domestic and partner violence, assault and battery, homicide, hit and run accidents, rural vandalism, and farm theft is reiterated by several studies (Parliament of Victoria Drugs and Crime Prevention Committee 2004; WHO 2007; Klingemann 2001).

Mortality and morbidity, exposure to HIV/AIDS, and crime and violence all have multiple socio-economic consequences. These include such problems as absenteeism from work, lack of capacity to work, job loss, and diminished capacity to play parental roles, disturbance of public peace, as well as increased pressure on human and material resources of the police, health care, and other social service agencies (Kelleher and Robbins 1997; Parliament of Victoria Drugs and Crime Prevention Committee 2004; WHO 2007; Klingemann 2001).

The study has established the existence of multiple direct and indirect negative impacts of heavy *aräqe* consumption that are manifested on the drinkers themselves as well as other community members. The direct consequences of *aräqe* consumption include social problems such as crime and violence, family violence and disruption; mental and physical health problems; and numerous economic impacts. The indirect/opportunity costs of *aräqe* consumption mainly include those arising out of crime and violence and ill-health of consumers.

The following section discusses each of these consequences on the basis of data collected mainly through FGDs with community leaders, in-depth interviews with health service providers and police officials, as well as the analysis of documented sources.

6.2.1 Crime and Violence

Crimes against property constitute the first category of crime identified by respondents as being caused or aggravated by *aräqe* consumption. The first of this type of crimes is theft. According to police officials, most criminals convicted of theft were those caught in the act while intoxicated. Moreover, many of these were repeat offenders who relied on continued stealing in order to finance their addiction to *aräqe*. The theft of household items, livestock, and other property fuelled by *aräqe* were all reported as common problems in the study sites. Extreme cases were reported by informants in rural Dämbäč'a, where *aräqe* addiction and the related spending has resulted in such criminal acts as the theft of sheaves of grain that were collected from fields and kept on the threshing floor. A second type of crime falling in this category is the destruction of property, including household furniture and equipment as well as *aräqe* selling items, by drunken family members and customers. Once again, the burning of a pile of crop sheaves, an excessive act of property destruction, was reported by interviewees in rural Dämbäč'a.

Assault and battery, involuntary manslaughter, and homicide constitute the second category of crimes, namely, crimes against the person. By far the commonest of all are brawls which involve threats or attempt to inflict bodily harm. An instance described by an elderly FGD participant in Qäyït illustrates this very well:

> A few years back, I was an armed *Qäbäle* militiaman. One day, as I was walking to the next village to run a certain errand, carrying a rifle, I came across a relative of mine with whom I had an old dispute over land. Unfortunately, that man was tipsy on *aräqe* and he started showering me with insults with a clear intent of provoking me to a fight, which I ignored and went my way. On my way back, that man, who was now even more drunk, accosted me and

threatened to attack me, daring me to use my gun if I were man enough. Luckily, I managed to control myself and left without falling into the trap.

Regrettably, not all confrontations end like the one presented above. Usually verbal insults and minor conflicts escalate into full blown fights, especially if the parties involved happen to hold grudges against one another. Such violent fights result in both light and heavy injuries upon the fighting parties, people who try to break the fight, or even innocent bystanders.

The problem was found to be most severe in Sululta, where such fights are said to be customary by almost all informants. In the words of an informant in the locality, "He who doesn't turn around after drinking, burns up!" (በጥቱ ያልተገለበጠ ያራል!). Data obtained through interviews of health center workers in Sululta show the seriousness of the problem in the *Wäräda*. In the year 2008/09 (2001 EC), the health center handled 2,729 (1748 male and 981 female) cases of fight-related injuries. Health service providers estimate 85% of these injuries to be a result of *aräqe* related-fights. In the same year, the *Wäräda* Police Station compiled 132 case files and started law suits of aggravated assault and battery against the 202 individuals involved. It is worth mentioning that according to informants in Sululta such brawls are not always individual incidences, rather cases of mass fights that occur at market places, mourning homes, and weddings, making the injury toll very high. A recent occurrence in Sululta where a fight that broke out in a mourning home caused the light injury of eight adults and fatal wounding of a four-year old child.

Though not as grave as Sululta, both Däbrä Bïrhan and Dämbäč'a have their own share of cases of assault and battery. Informants in both sites reported that fights that break out between people, usually with a history of previous conflicts, result in the injury of one or more persons. These fights by and large occur at market places and city entry/exit points as well as during wedding ceremonies and in mourning homes. In Däbrä Bïrhan, for instance, a study conducted by the town police station with the aim of reducing crime rate in the city found *aräqe* to be the primary cause of most crimes. This is especially true regarding fights that break out between migrant workers who have moved to the town following the recent boom in construction. Similarly, an informant from the Qäyït Sub-*Wäräda* Police Station explains that most of the cases of assault and battery they have investigated (115 from 2005/06 to 2008/09) were crimes committed by drunken perpetrators.

Čäha is the study site least affected by *aräqe*-related violence, as attested by quantitative data obtained from the police and health center as well as in-depth interviews with community members.

Interviews with informants further revealed that intoxication with *aräqe* is associated with a significant proportion of acts of homicide committed in the study areas. Reckless handling of firearms while drunk has resulted in the death of some, usually under shocking circumstances. In this regard, informants in Č'anč'o pointed out two cases: an instance where a best man was shot dead at a wedding by a person drunk on *aräqe*, and another where the bridegroom, under the influence of *aräqe*, accidentally shot and killed one of the invitees[20]. In addition to deaths from gunshot wounds, informants mentioned several cases where people were beaten or stabbed to death during fights involving *aräqe* in one way or another.

Note that there is a marked difference in the level of *aräqe*-related violence between sites. It tends to decrease as one goes from Sululta to Däbrä Bïrhan and then to Dämbäč'a, ending with Čäha. However, the fact that only a minority of cases are reported to the police/officials, the rest being handled by the *ïdïr*s in the case of Čäha is noteworthy.

6.2.2 Domestic Violence and Family Dissolution

When asked about the relation between *aräqe* consumption and domestic violence, informants stated the presence of a strong connection between the two. A drunken husband batters his wife and/or children, or engages in verbal attacks, insulting, shouting at and treating members of his family. Fights often break out between partners as a result of the squandering of household resources or inability to properly carry out responsibilities. An officer of the Sululta Police Station described the situation as follows: "The impacts of *aräqe* consumption on the family are multiple. Wife abuse – from minor ones such as verbal attacks to serious acts of wife beating – has its roots in *aräqe*. I personally remember a man who, while drunk, hit his wife with an ax, causing her serious injury."

Informants have also cited a few cases of family dissolution as a result of the addiction of wives to *aräqe*. According to informants, the relative improvement in women's social status as well as having their say on property management has allowed them to participate in the public sphere, visiting public places including those where *aräqe* is consumed, thereby exposing them to the same risks.

Quantitative evidence from other countries shows the gravity of this particular problem. Kelleher and Robbins (2000, 199-200), in their summary of extensive literature on alcohol and family-related problem in America, indicate

---

[20] In the celebrated case of the young girl who killed her husband-to-be in order to free herself from the clutches of her brutal abductors, the latter were well fortified by *aräqe* that was generously served to them by a female relative of theirs — as immortalized by the BBC-EWLA television program on her case.

that more than 60% of individuals with a diagnosis of alcohol abuse or dependence report family conflicts due to drinking. They further provide evidence indicating that as high as 50% of spouse-abuse cases involving police are associated with alcohol abuse.

The most defenseless victims of *aräqe* consumption in a family where there is an abuser are children. Not only are they neglected and physically abused by drunken parents, they also get to bear the emotional burden of witnessing their parents fight, which is likely to leave a permanent psychological scar. The final result of frequent conflicts is family split —separation, divorce, or children running away from home.

6.2.3 Health of Consumers

The health status of *aräqe* consumers is a function of not only the amount they drink over time and the frequency of their drinking, but also that of the general content, potency and quality of the drink. The study has found that the production of *aräqe* in Ethiopia is not regulated at all. As a result, its alcohol content, quality, as well as the type and proportion of its ingredients are highly variable. The only thing that one can be certain of *aräqe* is regarding its high alcohol content. Thus, this nature of its production, which it shares with those of traditional alcoholic drinks in other developing countries, has an important implication for the health status of consumers, a fact supported by a WHO finding (2004), which considers unregulated production of traditional alcohol throughout the developing world to be the culprit behind most of its harmful consequences.

Alcohol Dependence
The dependence producing qualities of alcoholic drinks in general are well documented by laboratory as well as field studies. According to WHO, alcohol is a substance that "has the capacity to produce a state of dependence, and central nervous system stimulation or depression, resulting in hallucinations or disturbances in motor function or thinking or behavior or perception or mood" (WHO 2007, 7).

The study's attempt to find out the harmful impact of *aräqe* consumption on those who drink has revealed results that point to the above described problem of alcohol dependency. Symptoms described include behavior considered improper by other community members such as drinking alone, making up excuses to drink, or drinking too much at once; failure to keep personal hygiene; preferring drinking over eating; extreme violence when drunk; and needing *aräqe* to function properly.

Informants also described behavioral patterns that are usually displayed by frequent *aräqe* drinkers when they are deprived of *aräqe*, i.e., what are commonly known as withdrawal symptoms. The most commonly cited of these was the shaking of one's body, but additional symptoms such as nervousness, confusion, and loss of appetite were also pointed out.

As described by respondents, individuals displaying such behavior continue to consume *aräqe* despite attempts by friends and relatives to make them give up drinking, often with disastrous physical, psychological, social and economic consequences.

Other studies provide quantitative data on the problem of alcohol dependence. Abebaw, Atalay and Hanlon (2007, 49), for instance, point out that the alcohol dependence rate in Ethiopia goes as high as 1.6% of the population for selected cities and rural areas, making it a very serious problem of the society.

Physical and Mental Health Issues
It is a well established fact that long term consumption of alcohol has acute and chronic health consequences. In line with this, the study has attempted to find out if any physical health related impacts of *aräqe* consumption were observed by community members and health workers. Surprisingly consistent responses were obtained from lay informants as well as health service providers.

When asked to indicate the negative health consequences of *aräqe* on frequent consumers, FGD participants listed liver disease, gastritis, 'lung disease', weight loss, eye problems, and general susceptibility to diseases. As can be expected, more refined responses were obtained from health professionals, who listed alcoholic liver diseases such as cirrhosis, gastric ulcer, respiratory tract infections, heart problems, and reduced immunity as being the common health problems faced by frequent *aräqe* consumers.

Abbink's findings regarding the felt impacts of *aräqe* among the people of the Maji area support the above. He writes,

> All informants from the Surma, Me'en and Dixi agree to the statement that constant problems of drunkenness (and even of liver-disease) started in the last fifteen to twenty years (for the Surma even much more recent: only since around 1989) in their societies, when *katikala* [i.e. *aräqe*] production and consumption increased markedly (1997, 17).

The study made a similar attempt to investigate the mental health-related impacts of prolonged *aräqe* consumption. While lay respondents described these impacts in general terms such as 'they go crazy', health care professionals explained that depression and anxiety (a sense of dissatisfaction, unhappiness or restlessness) are highly correlated with *aräqe* abuse.

In an attempt to broaden the scope of the study as regards the mental health-related impact of *aräqe* and also check on the validity of what has been learnt from informants in the study areas, a visit was made to the Department of Psychiatry of the Medical School of Addis Ababa University. An in-depth interview was conducted with Dr. Solomon Teferra, who is a practicing clinical psychiatrist specializing in alcohol-related mental illness. According to Dr. Solomon, most of the patients he has treated over the years have had problem with alcohol in general and some 70% with *aräqe* in particular. He emphasized the fact that the number of patients that indulge in *yä abäša aräqe* dominates the field of alcohol consumption, and is on the rise, which he attributed to its potency and low price. Going further into the dynamics of choice and dependence, he indicated the fact that his patients generally descend into the cheapest and most potent type of alcoholic drink, *aräqe*, as they sink deeper into the vicious cycle of dependence, inability to perform and lack of financial resources. This he illustrated with the examples of even professionals that went down the same route (see Box 7 for one such case).

Box 7: Sliding Down the Liquor Ladder

In the course of his interview, Dr Solomon related the real life story of one well placed professional whose case he had followed. This person had become alcohol dependant to the extent of being incapable of undertaking the tasks involved in his daily routine and work. Then, as he sank deeper and deeper into alcohol dependence, he reached the point at which he could not afford to support his habit without sliding down the liquor ladder. The more alcohol dependent he became, the more the amount of liquor he needed, and the higher the bill he had to foot. He therefore gave up first on the high priced imported spirits such as whisky, gin, and cognac, and then even on the medium priced local factory products. Thus, gradually, this well educated professional ended up being a fulltime patron of *aräqe* that was the cheapest while most potent alcoholic beverage available. As time went by, he had had to take along with him his daily supply of the colorless stuff to his workplace disguising it as bottled water lest it be detected by his colleagues and clients.

Dr Solomon categorized the patients that were treated for problems relating to alcohol into two. The first kind of patients are those that were treated for alcohol dependence. This category of patients were treated in order to be rehabilitated from *alcohol dependence* since, (a) intoxication has the immediate impact of impairing their perception and judgment; (b) sudden and unsupervised withdrawal can also lead to serious physical and mental health problems; (c) since it also leads to a plethora of physical and mental problems if alcohol dependence is left to continue. The second reasons for which patients are treated are what are known as *alcohol induced mental illnesses* that include psychosis, acute anxiety and depression.

HIV and AIDS

The role of alcohol in HIV transmission was stressed by informants in both rural and urban areas of the study sites. Even though the risk seems to be much higher in urban areas where *aräqe* selling and commercial sex work go hand in hand in specialized districts such as Däboqa of Č'anč'o in Sululta *Wäräda*, Katanga of Däbrä Bïrhan, and Tägulät Säfär of Qäyït, the risk is also carried over to the rural areas, as a significant proportion of the patrons of such places are rural married men.

According to informants, patrons of *aräqe taverns* often engage in extramarital sex with multiple partners, and under a state of drunkenness and reduced capacity of judgment, they fail to properly use condoms. According to an informant in Sululta, common sayings in the Č'anč'o town's red light district include: "There is no HIV after 6:00 PM!" (ከ12 ሰዓት በኋላ ኤች.አይ.ቪ. የለም!); "After 6:00 PM we wouldn't be scared of HIV, even if it itself comes in a dress!" (ከ12 ሰዓት በኋላ ኤች.አይ.ቪ. ራሱ እንኳን ቀሚስ ለብሶ ቢመጣ አንፈራውም!). Unfortunately, unsuspecting victims of such risky behavior are rural women, whose husbands frequent the *aräqe tavern*-cum-brothels, often with little regard for safety.

Accidents

The causal role of alcohol consumption in accidents is well documented by experimental and field studies. Particularly, the capacity of alcoholic drinks to reduce judgment and motor skill is a main causal factor for the occurrence of injuries resulting from falls, mishandling of equipment, and traffic accidents. Data on African countries on the issue of alcohol consumption and accidents indicate that, on the average, nearly half of hospital-treated cases of accident injuries involve patients who have consumed alcohol at the time of the accident (Room *et al.* 2002, 140-143).

As *aräqe* is a potent alcoholic drink, its capacity to reduce judgment and motor skill, when drunk in excess, is very high. Accordingly, the study attempted to see if *aräqe*-related accidents have occurred in the study site. Accidents of different levels of seriousness were reported by informants. These include drunken people that were hit and killed by car, fell off a bridge and died, and fell over a cliff. Informants from Sululta police office listed three cases of hit and ran where all the victims had been seen exiting *aräqe taverns* or being visibly drunk before they were killed.

Failure to Follow Treatment
In-depth interviews with health professionals regarding the problems they encounter as a result of *aräqe* consumption by their clients showed that failures to cooperate during treatment and follow prescriptions afterwards are the most serious of such problems.

Medical professionals stated that it is difficult to care for drunken patients (who are in the health center usually to be treated for injuries from *aräqe* related fights) because such patients often resist anesthetic, become violent, move around/fidget a lot, or even throw away bandages.

Moreover, patients, particularly those who have developed *aräqe* dependence, fail to follow instructions given by medical professionals. Failure to take medication, drinking while taking medication, and failure to maintain proper personal hygiene are the most common problems listed by informants. The study also found that, despite repeated medical advice, many people following antiretroviral therapy consume *aräqe* rendering the drug less effective and even running the risk of developing drug-resistant strains of the HIV virus.

Writing on a similar problem in three African countries, Morris *et al.* cite extensive sources which demonstrate that alcohol consumption can actually reduce drug compliance and efficacy. They further point out to the greater threat of the breeding of drug-resistant strains of HIV as a result of reduced compliance with treatment (2006, 171).

Aräqe Adulteration, Hygiene, and Their Potential for Disease Transmission
In addition to the actual health hazards posed by *aräqe*, its disease-causing potential needs to be noted. One source of such risk is the additives (such as *indod, ye midir imbuway*) that are said to be added in the course of its production in order to increase its potency. Even though the study has not uncovered evidence regarding injuries or deaths that are attributed to adulteration, this could be due to informants' inability to extract the impact of additives from the intricate impact of *aräqe* on people's health. As the evidence from research on impact of additives (some of which contain highly poisonous substances such as lead and arsenic) on the health of traditional alcohol consumers conducted on

other developing countries regularly indicate, they are sources of significant number of deaths (Room *et al.* 2002)[21].

Another risk factor is the rather unhygienic production and marketing process (exchanging of numerous hands and at inappropriate sites without regard for cleanliness), which could have made *aräqe* a virtual death trap. Apparently, distillation and high alcohol content that makes it an effective detergent counteract the possibility of disease transmission that should have resulted from the latter risk factor.

6.3 Direct Economic Impacts

The study has found out that *aräqe* consumption has economic costs that are felt directly. Even though in most cases these costs are incurred by the drinker and his/her immediate family, the wider community, of which the drinker is a member, is also quite often implicated. The sections below present the direct economic impacts of *aräqe* consumption in greater detail.

Depletion of Cash Savings, Food and Seed Grains and Other Assets
The direct economic impact of *aräqe* consumption is felt the most in terms of money spent directly on *aräqe* consumption thus leading to the depletion of cash saving, food, seed grains and other assets.

The research confirmed the obvious fact that habitual consumers of *aräqe* are known for their excessive spending on *aräqe* and failure to save any meaningful amount. The squandering of cash borrowed from saving and credit associations is stated as a serious problem, along with the sale of food and seed grain, calves, and eucalyptus logs. Some extreme cases were raised in rural Dämbäč'a, where the problem appears to be more ominous (see Box 8).

While the depletion of cash savings, food, seed grains[22] and other assets is a serious problem in itself, its role as a source of marital conflicts and spouse abuse is also stressed by respondents in all of the study sites.

---

[21] A case in point is Kenya, where in 2002 the consumption of home-fermented beverage called *kumi kumi* killed 140 people and blinded many others in places known as Mukuru Kwa Njenga and Mukuru Kaiyaba (WHO 2004).

[22] Note that the focuses of this particular section are the impacts of *aräqe* consumption, and that those of *aräqe* production on food grains are dealt with under Section 4.3.3.

Box 8: The Downward Spiral Caused by *Aräqe* Related Spending

In the course of the FGD with the community leaders of Yäshäboč *Qäbäle* of Dämbäč'a, the issue of the economic impact of *aräqe* consumption was raised. The following is what an elder stated forcefully, to the satisfaction of all other participants:

> There are people in our *Qäbäle* who have spent on *aräqe* more than half of the money they borrowed from the Amhara Saving and Credit Association on the very day they got it, and a few of them do not even have a change of cloth. There are also those that have sold their houses, livestock, and even land. The owner of that land for instance [pointing to a plot covered with crop] rented it out to someone before the beginning of the year. He has now spent all the money he received on *aräqe* and has again rented out the land for next year even before the harvest on it is collected.

Further discussion with other participants and separate in-depth interviews with key informants also confirmed what was said by the elder.

Diminished Interest and Physical Capacity for Work

The economic impact of *aräqe* goes beyond the money directly spent on its purchase, as it also reduces the earning capacity of those who drink it. People who are dependent on *aräqe* spend a significant amount of their time looking for and consuming *aräqe*, ignoring farm work/management.

According to informants, people who drink *aräqe* do little work on Mondays and on days after a market day because the days before provide plenty of opportunity for *aräqe* consumption. Informants further explained that the hangover from *aräqe* drinking is so bad that the day after, one can't even stand by oneself let alone do farm work. The phrases employed by some of the respondents to describe the state of individuals suffering from *aräqe* hangover, such as, "it makes one beg for water" and "it makes one crawl like a baby", illustrate this point very well.

Failure to Participate in Development Schemes and Extension Packages

The strongest complaints regarding *aräqe* consumption and its impact on participation in development schemes come from agricultural development agents in the study areas, who stated that addiction to *aräqe* has made many farmers forgetful and reluctant to engage in development activities. Since farmers flock en mass to the nearby towns in search of *aräqe*, any meaningful implementation of extension packages is difficult. More specifically, the study found that the widespread and frequent consumption of *aräqe* has negative impacts on development activities carried out by NGOs as well as microfinance extension agencies, as loans/aid given to people are often spent on *aräqe*. Such, for instance, was the case with the NGO *Hunde* that has worked for a number of years in the Sululta area. According to the Executive Director of the NGO, Ato Zegeye Asfaw, the beneficiaries of one of its projects in the *Wäräda* had gone to the extent of deciding at their general assembly to ban the consumption of *aräqe* among its members and to discourage it among members of the community at large.

6.4 Indirect and Opportunity Costs of Äräqe Consumption

In addition to the readily felt direct costs of *aräqe* consumption, there are indirect and opportunity costs, particularly due to crime and violence, and ill health. These indirect costs mainly relate to the productive activities that are not performed by the consumers of *aräqe* as well as the labor time wasted on handling the adverse consequences of drinking.

As described in Section 6.2.1 and 6.2.2, *aräqe*-related conflicts and family disturbances are common in most of the study sites. One major indirect consequence of these is the **loss of labor time** by the conflicting parties and those mediating *aräqe*-related conflicts.

The many casualties of *aräqe*-related fights and accidents all have to spend a considerable amount of time getting treated and recovering from their injuries, again wasting valuable productive time. In addition to the injured, there are the friends and family who carry or accompany them to the health centers, sacrificing hours of working time.

In situations where attempts are made by village elders to resolve such conflicts, several lengthy meetings need to be held. These meetings engage for hours several people (three or more elders, witnesses, the conflicting parties, as well as their family members and close kin/friends) whose labor-time could have been spent on other productive activities. Ironically, at the conclusion of reconciliation, the whole party moves together to a tavern "in order to effectively seal the peace agreement with *aräqe*." Alas, it is not uncommon, we were informed, for some among such a peace-making party to exceed their limits by a glass too many and get into fights thereby rekindling the vicious circle of drinking and fighting.

However, not all conflicts are solved by traditional mediations. Many actually go to the police and eventually the courts. Here also, conflicting parties spend from a few hours to a few weeks under police custody until the case is presented to the courts. In addition, witnesses spend precious time and money traveling to a police station/court, giving testimony, etc.

Additional workload on the civil service institutions, namely, the police, courts and local administration, is another indirect consequence felt both by the community and the aforementioned bodies. The workload of police officers is significantly increased, particularly on market days and holidays, often necessitating the use of extra officers to patrol the streets and villages well into the evening, stretching resources to their limits. In addition to the police, town/*qäbäle* administrations have also to make constant efforts to prevent the *aräqe* marketing and consumption related disturbances/crimes.

Once criminal acts are committed, the burden of investigation falls on the police, who stressed the fact that *aräqe* is involved in most criminal cases they handle. Of course, the courts that handle these cases also spend considerable time on account of *aräqe*, which could have been utilized to administer justice on other cases.

According to informants working in the health centers in the study sites, handling *aräqe* related cases takes up much of their time, particularly during market days. Often on such days, health care workers are required to **work overtime or extra hands are called in** to assist just to cope with the large inflow of patients. Not only does this increase public spending, it also prevents health care workers from concentrating their efforts on the best thing they could do—take care of other patients.

As already described in Section 6.1.3 of this paper, it is customary to consume *aräqe* on social occasions such as *yä fint'ïr, yä däsdäs, täzkar, jïgi/däbo* as well as *ïrq*. Such social drinking sometimes spirals out of control and leads to heated arguments and fights, often disrupting the very function it was supposed to facilitate. Moreover, informants have cited individuals who, due to their *aräqe* consumption habits, repeatedly defaulted on payment of *ïdïr* and *ïqub* fees. In the case of the former, default on payment resulting in the expulsion of the nonpayer, and in the case of the latter, in the guarantor of the defaulter being made to foot the unpaid bill.

6.5 The Cumulative Impact of Aräqe Consumption on Society

The above discussed negative impacts of *aräqe* consumption in Ethiopia tend to combine multiplicatively to immense societal distress. No wonder that a study done for WHO states the social costs of alcohol consumption goes up to 3% of gross domestic product of a nation. While about 20% of the total costs are direct costs, representing the amount actually spent on medical, social and judicial services, about 10% of the total costs are spent on material damage, and about 70% of the total costs represent lost earnings of individuals who die prematurely or are unable to perform their productive tasks in the way they would have if they had not been consuming alcohol (Klingemann 2001, 9).

As the bulk of alcoholic beverages consumed in Ethiopia are traditional drinks, and since *aräqe* has by far the highest alcohol content of all homebrewed alcoholic beverages, it arguably accounts for the lion's share of the negative impacts of alcohol consumption in the country in general.

VII. Local and National Measures for Regulating Alcohol

Finally, the study has looked into attempts at discouraging aräqe consumption, undertaken by state organs and community-based organizations (CBOs) at the local level, as well as into the state of national policy and institutional environment for the regulation of alcohol.

7.1 Local-Level Counter-Measures

Community-Based Organizations and traditional institutions have here and there taken some uncoordinated action against the widespread and rising *aräqe* consumption. In Sululta, Däbrä Bïrhan and Čäha, parish churches have successfully banned *aräqe* from their premises. Such a measure was not necessary in Dämbäč'a as *aräqe* was never consumed on church grounds in the first place.

Čäha is exceptional in involving *ïdïrs* in placing proscription against drunkenness by imposing a fine. Likewise, in Dämbäč'a, the police catch and jail drunkards who disturb the peace and wellbeing of the community, taking them to their respective parish churches on Sunday where they face their fellow parishioners and made to pay a fine of 25 Birr. This latter case, it should be noted, is instructive of how a government organ (the police) and traditional institutions (parish churches) can cooperate effectively.

The few actions that have been taken by local authorities to date are mainly directed at dealing with the symptoms rather than at wrestling with *aräqe* consumption itself. Thus, in all of the study sites, emphasis is being placed on reducing the level of crime and traffic accidents in general, including those that are due to *aräqe* consumption, through the implementation of the Community Policing Program and more vigilant traffic control. Likewise, in a related move, the administration of *Qäbäle* 02 of Däbrä Bïrhan town has organized 13 women whose livelihood was previously based on distilling *aräqe* into an association that it has made in charge of running the compound for parking pack animals located close to the town's main marketplace.

The Qäyït *qäbäle* administration stands out as an exception among the state administrative organs in the study areas for taking a measure, albeit a very weak one, to discourage *aräqe* consumption. The Chairman and Vice-chairman of the *qäbäle* insisted that they regularly advise *aräqe* retailers not to sell *aräqe* to already tipsy would-be customers.

In all of the study sites, an indirect negative pressure was found being applied on the production and marketing of *aräqe*. The Micro-Finance Extension

Program is forbidden to support activities such as *aräqe* and *č'at* production and marketing that are termed *non-developmental activities* through the provision of credit. Similarly, at least in some of the study sites such as Qäyït, applicants who are known to be *aräqe* dependant are automatically disqualified from taking loans from the Micro-Finance Extension Program.

7.2 Developments in the Policy and Institutional Environment for the Regulation of Alcohol

As far as international agreements go, Ethiopia is a signatory of all three UN conventions on narcotics and psychotropic substances (NPS)[23]. These are the Single Convention on Narcotic Drugs of 1961 that could not ban the many newly discovered psychotropics, since its scope was limited to drugs with cannabis-, coca-, and opium-like effects; the Convention on Psychotropic Substances that was worded to include almost any conceivable mind-altering substances of 1971; and, the United Nations Convention Against Illicit Traffic in Narcotic Drugs and Psychotropic Substances of 1988 (United Nations 1961, 1971, 1988). The last-mentioned convention, which is the most comprehensive of all three, has four schedules of controlled substances that, taken together, include the whole spectrum of NPS from dangerous drugs and synthetic hallucinogens to stimulants of the amphetamine type to barbiturate products to hypnotics, tranquillizers and analgesics1988 (United Nations 1988).

These UN conventions are based on the distinction between substances that are to be *controlled* and those that are only to be *regulated*. A substance is said to be controlled if its production, supply, stock management, distribution, use, and disposal are restricted and governed by law, and any infringement of the

---

[23] According to Encarta, *psychotropic drugs* is the generic term by which drugs developed from *psychoactive substances* that alter mood, behavior, perception, or mental functioning and used to treat patients with severe mental illness are known in current professional practice.

> Alcohol has always been the most widely used psychoactive substance. In most countries it is the only psychoactive drug legally available without prescription. Pleasant relaxation is commonly the desired effect, but intoxication impairs judgment and motor performance. When used chronically, alcohol can be toxic to liver and brain cells and can be physiologically addicting (giving rise to alcoholism), producing dangerous withdrawal syndromes (Microsoft Encarta 2006).

latter is considered an offence with legal consequences. Thus narcotics and psychotropic drugs are controlled substances governed by the UN conventions. On the other hand, a substance is said to be regulated if its production, supply, stock management, distribution, use, or disposal is guided by rules and regulations that a country sees fit to impose. Accordingly, all medicine, be it prescription medicine or one that is sold over the counter, is subject to government regulation, and therefore falls within the category of regulated substance. The d decision on what and how to regulate a substance is left to individual countries.

The three UN conventions on NPS do not classify alcohol as a substance to be controlled, which could because of the lesser requirement for the treatment that its addiction involves or due to the wide social acceptability it enjoys. Furthermore, these conventions do not even provide for the regulation of alcohol leaving it to individual member states to act as they see fit.

The national policy and legal environment, too, remained equally unfavorable for the regulation of alcohol until very recently. Up until the beginning of the current calendar year, Ethiopia had two national policies and one proclamation potentially relevant to the control, regulation, and administration of narcotics and psychotropic substances, drugs, health care, and food. These were: The National Drug Policy of the Transitional Government of Ethiopia, The Health Policy of the Transitional Government of Ethiopia, both of which were declared in 1993, and Proclamation No. 176/1999 Providing for Drug Administration and Control.

The National Drug Policy of the Transitional Government of Ethiopia, published in October 1993, deals only with narcotic and psychotropic drugs. In this regard, it specifically states that: (1) "[the government] shall make the necessary efforts to deter the illegal manufacturing, distribution and consumption of narcotics and psychotropic drugs"; (2) "Laws and regulations shall be instituted and enforced governing the supply, stock management, distribution, use, and disposal of narcotic and psychotropic drugs"; and (3) "a national committee consisting of different organizations shall be set up to carry out a coordinated control on narcotic and psychotropic drugs on the basis of international conventions" (Transitional Government of Ethiopia 1993a). Nowhere in this policy document are alcohol and č'at mentioned, let alone discussed.

The Health Policy of the Transitional Government of Ethiopia, proclaimed in September 1993, does not deal with any aspects of alcohol, tobacco, or č'at. None of its articles make mention of these substances (Transitional Government of Ethiopia 1993b).

Proclamation No. 176/1999, a Proclamation to Provide for Drug Administration and Control that entered into force on 29 June 1999 established the Drug Administration and Control Authority, with duties and powers over the administration and control of drugs including NPS (Federal Negarit Gazeta – No. 60, 29th June, 1999). The Proclamation does not venture into the realm of food and drinks as it was not meant to do so, and consequently makes also no mention of alcohol, *aräqe*, and *č'at*.

Thus, until very recently all the potentially relevant policy and legislative instruments of the country were completely silent on issues of alcohol and *č'at*, and included no provisions that could be interpreted to imply their regulation.

As of recently, however, the international and national legal and institutional landscape on alcohol have changed significantly, making the regulation of some alcohol not only feasible but also mandatory. Within a brief period of half a year, from mid-January to mid-July 2010, a spate of international and national policy and legislative developments that are capable of reformatting the policy and institutional environment for reducing the harmful use of alcohol, including those of the illicit and informally/traditionally produced ones such as *aräqe*, have taken effect.

At its sixty-third World Health Assembly held on 20 May 2010 in Geneva, the 193 Member States of the World Health Organization (WHO) adopted in a consensus vote the *Global Strategy to Reduce the Harmful Use of Alcohol*. Thus, an international convention on alcohol that will guide the policies and actions of individual countries at the same time as it helps coordinate their collective effort is in place for the first time ever.

The Global Strategy to Reduce the Harmful Use of Alcohol that was prepared with the participation of 149 Member States clarifies its primary objective of giving direction to, and facilitating the work of national governments and institutions, particularly through the first article of its section on *National Policies and Measures*, which reads as follows:

> The harmful use of alcohol can be reduced if effective actions are taken by countries to protect their populations. Member States have a primary responsibility for formulating, implementing, monitoring and evaluating public policies to reduce the harmful use of alcohol. Such policies require a wide range of public health-oriented strategies for prevention and treatment. All countries will benefit from having a national strategy and appropriate legal frameworks to reduce harmful use of alcohol, regardless of the level of resources in the country. Depending on the characteristics of policy options and national circumstances, some policy options can be implemented by non-legal frameworks such as guidelines or voluntary restraints. Successful implementation of measures should be assisted by monitoring impact and compliance and establishing and imposing sanctions for non-compliance with adopted laws and regulations (WHO 2010, 9).

The fourth article under the section *National Policies and Measures* lists 10 recommended target areas into which the policy options and interventions available for national action can be grouped. These target areas that should be seen as mutually supportive and complementary are:

(a) Leadership, awareness and commitment, (b) Health services' response, (c) Community action, (d) Drink-driving policies and countermeasures, (e) Availability of alcohol, (f) Marketing of alcoholic beverages, (g) Pricing policies, (h) Reducing the negative consequences of drinking and alcohol intoxication, (i) Reducing the public health impact of illicit alcohol and informally produced alcohol, (j) Monitoring and surveillance (WHO 2010, 10).

As far as Ethiopia is concerned, the Global Strategy comes at a very opportune moment. It coincides with three significant legislative and institutional measures the country has recently taken. Firstly, an important legislation, namely, Proclamation No. 661/2009 to Provide for Food, Medicine and Health Care Administration and Control, was passed on 13 January 2010, among other things, in order:

… to protect the public from health risks emerging out of unsafe and poor quality food;

… to make the fragmented and poor quality administrative and regulatory system in the health sector efficient and effective, [and]…to establish a new and coordinated food, medicines and health care regulatory system (Federal Negarit Gazeta 2010, Preamble)

Secondly, following the provisions of the same Proclamation for the establishment of an appropriate "executive agency", the Food, Medicine, Health Care Administration and Control Authority (FMHACA), was set up replacing the old Drug Administration and Control Authority (DACA) as of 9 July 2010. Thirdly, acting on the basis of the provisions made by Proclamation No. 661/2009, FMHACA set itself to develop various regulations and working modalities for the administration of food, medicine, and health care, which it has already submitted to the Council of Ministers for approval.

Proclamation No. 661/2009, which constitutes a complete overhaul over the previously declared two policies and Proclamation No. 176/1999 as regards alcohol, does not, however, address it explicitly, and fails to deal with *č'at* even implicitly. Yet the "open-ended" definitions of "food" and "food trade", which read as follows, provide the FMHACA with enough legal room within which to work out a scheme for the regulation of alcohol in general and *aräqe* in particular:

"food" means any raw, semi-processed or processed substance for commercial purpose or to be served for the public in any way intended for human consumption that includes water and other drinks, chewing gum, supplementary food and any substance which has been used in the manufacture, preparation or treatment of food, but does not include tobacco and substances used only as medicines" (Federal Negarit Gazeta 2010, Article 2 Sub-article 1)

"food trade" means production, preparation, irradiation, export, import, storage, distribution, transport, wholesale and retail of food and food raw materials for commercial purposes and includes the provision of food quality control laboratory service (Federal Negarit Gazeta 2010, Article 2 Sub-article 2).

The Proclamation makes provisions for the safety and quality control as well as the packaging and labeling of what it defines as food in the following terms:

No food or its raw material, additive or packaging material shall be put into use unless it complies with the international and national safety and quality standards (Federal Negarit Gazeta 2010, Article 7 Sub-article 1).

Any producer, importer, distributor or retailer of packed food shall not supply it to the market or distribute it otherwise unless it is duly packed and labeled (Federal Negarit Gazeta 2010, Article 8 Sub-article 1).

Proclamation 661/2010 gives the power of setting standards in relation to food, medicine, etc., as well as that of "licensing and regulating trans-regional food and medicine production, import, export, distribution, promotion and storage of food and medicine and quality control laboratory" to the federal executive organ (Federal Negarit Gazeta 2010, Article 3 Sub-article 2 a and b). On the other hand, the Proclamation identifies the role of regional states by stating that "other regulatory activities which are not given to the Executive organ [i.e., FMHACA] ... shall be carried out by states government regulatory bodies" (Federal Negarit Gazeta 2010, Article 3 Sub-article 3).

Thus, FMHACA is currently the sole federal executive authority in charge of food, medicine and healthcare, administration and control, all responsibility in this regard has been moved from its precursor the Drug Administration and Control Authority (DACA) as well as from the Ministry of Health. As the federal level regulator of alcohol, the Authority shall develop standards for regulating alcohol (including *aräqe*) and once these are approved, it will see to it that they are communicated to, followed and implemented by the regional and *wäräda* level bureaus and offices. FMHACA will also implement these regulations as they relate to inter-regional *aräqe* marketing.

FMHACA is also required to apply the provisions of the Global Strategy to Reduce the Harmful Use of Alcohol, to which Ethiopia is a signatory, since *aräqe* clearly falls within the category it calls "informally produced alcohol" and defines as, "alcoholic beverages produced at home or locally by fermentation and distillation of fruits, grains, vegetables and the like, and often within the context of local cultural practices and traditions" (WHO 2010, 10).

FMHACA is working towards regulating the bulk production of all alcohol including at the cottage industry level. To achieve this, it has developed a draft regulatory scheme that is currently under revision following the request of the Council of Ministers. As it goes through the processes of revision and approval, the draft regulation will be made to explicitly deal with cottage produced alcohol including *aräqe*, according to Ato Dawit Dikasso, the Deputy Director General of the Authority, who added that the adoption of the Global Strategy to Reduce the Harmful Use of Alcohol on 20 May 2010 creates a good opportunity for FMHACA to set up its alcohol regulatory scheme according to the percepts and overall directions provided by this global strategy to which Ethiopia is a signatory.

According to Ato Dawit, FMHACA considers any substance the alcoholic content of which is below 45-50% as "food". Hence, alcoholic drinks including *aräqe* fall within the category of "food", which is defined by Proclamation 661/2010 to include any drink and substance that is ingested other than tobacco. That squarely places their regulation within the mandate of FMHACA, which is currently engaged in developing a wide-ranging system that will include the regulation of alcoholic drinks that are traded. Whereas all alcoholic drinks that are produced and consumed within the household shall therefore remain outside government regulation, all food and drink that is produced in bulk for the market either in factories or cottage industries and traded will be subject to government regulation.

Ato Dawit went on to say, as the federal level regulator of alcohol, the Authority shall develop standards for regulating alcohol (including *aräqe*) and once these are approved, it will see to it that they are communicated to, followed and implemented by the regional and *wäräda* level bureaus and offices. The EFMHACA shall also implement these regulations as they relate to inter-regional *aräqe* marketing.

FMHACA is organized to undertake its activities through a Central Branch Office that is concerned with port inspection and regulation, and five Branch Offices located in five towns of the country. It also gets its activities underway through regional and *wäräda* level regulatory agencies or unit, while the team within the FMHACA that is exclusively responsible for food can be strengthened with professional staff and resources and be made specifically mandated to deal with the regulation of alcohol with special emphasis on *aräqe*, according to Ato Dawit.

At the regional level, regional regulatory agencies or units shall implement the regulations handed down to them from the federal Authority. They will be responsible for all implementation within their respective regions, save those that are inter-regional, as per Proclamation No. 661/2009. At the *wäräda* level, too, the *wäräda* regulatory units within health offices shall implement the regulations passed down to them from their respective regional regulatory agencies or units, according to Ato Dawit Dikasso.

Finally, a few words about *č'at* are in order. The three UN conventions on narcotics and psychotropic substances that Ethiopia has ratified do not classify *č'at* as a kind of drug to be controlled or regulated, although, in theory, *č'at* (and even alcohol) belongs to the category of psychotropic substances on account of its addictive power. Why it is left out by the conventions could be because of its lesser requirement for treatment or due to the wide social acceptability it enjoys, explained Ato Dawit. FMHACA, on its part, has not categorized *č'at* as a narcotic or psychotropic substance, and underlines the fact that even the theoretical association between *č'at* and NPS is mentioned for educational and not practical purposes, according to the same source. Therefore, *č'at* is thus not treated in any way and capacity by the government of Ethiopia. It is, to date, completely left out of all relevant state policies and proclamations to be dealt with only according to pragmatic considerations.

VIII. Conclusions and Recommendations

8.1 Synoptic Balance Sheet of the Pros and Cons

This study amply demonstrates that *aräqe* production and marketing have both positive and negative aspects. This is crystal clear particularly from the perspective and wellbeing of women, who are the major actors, and from the wellbeing and socioeconomic development of the communities in which it is produced. *Aräqe* production provides tens of thousands of women or more with the only opportunity of livelihood, and this is a very important matter. On the other hand, even its production has some negative aspects, namely:

i. *Aräqe* is commonly distilled by poor women who can only employ archaic, energy inefficient and polluting methods of production that affect their health and also contribute to the progressive denuding of the vegetation cover of the land.

ii. Judging on the basis of the amount of *aräqe* that is distilled throughout the country from fermented cereals that happen to be very important food grains, the contribution of its production to food insecurity at the household and community levels cannot be taken lightly.

Aräqe marketing plays a pivotal role in the growth of urban markets, expansion of the service sector, urban development including housing, and increase in municipal revenue. Moreover, its wholesale and retail trades are important sources of income to the women who make up the overwhelming majority of the participants. The retail trade in particular is a profitable undertaking for a large number of women that includes most distillers. However, this too comes at a price. It brings in its wake a number of difficulties, particularly the following:

i. It generally impacts negatively on children's education since homes where *aräqe* is retailed don't provide the right kind of environment where children can study and concentrate on their studies.

ii. It creates a fertile ground for marital conflict, especially in cases where the husband is a heavy drinker and therefore demands free access to the *aräqe* that is readied for sale.

iii. *Aräqe* taverns where the stuff is sold by the shot glass sometimes serve as prostitution and crime dens. In addition to their role as hotspots of HIV infection, they contribute to the disturbance of the public's peace and various sorts of illegal transactions.

The study's verdict on *aräqe* consumption is unambiguous. The harmful effects of *aräqe* consumption are long-lasting, and outstrip its ability to produce short-lived feelings of relaxation and delight on the individual. Even its usefulness in boosting the food and entertainment industry cannot compensate for its overall destructiveness. The following are a few of its most prominent negative consequences:

i. Due to its relatively recent introduction into the country, the consumption of *aräqe* has not been effectively woven into and regulated by local customs and community norms.

ii. *Aräqe* intoxication is the cause of widespread fights, criminal acts, and accidents, all of which disrupt the proper functioning of communities in which *aräqe* consumption is common.

iii. Due to its dependence producing properties, *aräqe* has rendered many habitual users incapable of carrying out their parental, familial, and societal, and other personal duties.

iv. Owing to its toxic properties, long-term consumption of *aräqe* causes an array of mental and physical illnesses, including cirrhosis, gastric ulcer, respiratory tract infections, heart problems as well as anxiety and depression.

v. The combined socioeconomic impacts of the above are felt in the form of increased workload on hospitals, the police, and the courts as well as resources and manpower spent on handling *aräqe*-related medical and public disorder problems.

In sum, it is quite obvious from what has been said in the foregoing paragraphs that as one moves from the production of *aräqe* to its marketing and finally to its consumption, benign effects gradually wane and disappear, being replaced by those that are totally and clearly malign. Thus, in spite of the seeming ambivalence on *aräqe* emerging from the study, it is important to realize the fact that the two sides of the equation do not at all weigh equally. The interrelated aspects of *aräqe* production, marketing, and consumption when taken together represent a phenomenon that is by and large negative and holds Ethiopian society in a vice-like grip from which it is unlikely to free itself completely.

8.2 The Way Forward

That there is no simple solution for the problems posed by *aräqe* ought to be recognized from the outset. Firstly, Ethiopian society is caught in a double bind regarding what to do with *aräqe* since any action or omission is likely to negatively impact on some of its segments. Secondly, getting rid of *aräqe* in a sweep by prohibiting and criminalizing its production, sale, or consumption is not a viable option, since such a draconian measure would be impossible to enforce due to the informal nature of the undertakings, the large number of people engaged in them, the geographical spread of the activities, as well as the complex logistics and huge financial costs that enforcing such a measure would involve. Thus, whichever way one looks at it, *aräqe* appears to be here to stay.

On the contrary, to leave the production, marketing, and consumption regime of *aräqe* in its current sate is not an acceptable alternative, considering all the negative aspects and impacts of *aräqe* that are laid bare by this study. Something will have to be done about it urgently. After weighing the impossibility of sweeping it away, on the one hand, and the unacceptability of its continuation in the present state and manner, on the other, what one can realistically hope for would be the regulation of *aräqe* with the ultimate objective of reducing its related problems.

Before getting down to the main task of sketching the outlines of our proposed roadmap, however, we need to emphasize yet another important assertion. Solutions for *aräqe*-related problems must be provided within the general framework of a wider scheme for alcohol in general. To try and target *aräqe* in isolation from other alcoholic drinks such as factory-distilled liquors would be both difficult and ineffective. It would be similar to shooting down a moving target, since the likelihood of the problems moving back and forth between different alcoholic beverages is real. But, on the other hand, there is a need to come up with specific solutions for *aräqe* due to the specificities of its production, marketing, and consumption. As the subject of this study is *aräqe*, our effort will therefore be focused on the latter without totally ignoring the former.

A distinction that is made by Room and his colleagues in respect to actions to reduce alcohol-related problems is useful in further preparing the ground for our identification of what can and should be done with *aräqe*. They write:

There are two categories of action to be considered: those that seek primarily to change individual behavior, and those that look to the environments surrounding individuals in the hope that changes at that level will alter the relationship between the drinker, the alcohol, and the complex of problems that can potentially result from interaction between the two (Room et al. 2002, 164).

8.2.1 Measures That Seek Primarily to Change Individual Behavior

The first of the above-mentioned categories, that which comprises actions that seek primarily to change individual behavior, includes: (a) anti-alcohol *education and persuasion campaigns*, (b) *deterrence*, i.e., the threat of negative sanctions or incentives for behavior, and (c) *treatment and other individualized help* that includes a variety of schemes such as *specialized alcohol treatment settings, management of alcohol problems in the workplace*, and *mutual-help organizations*. While it is necessary to integrate education and persuasion campaigns, deterrence, and treatment for alcoholic problems in the national scheme for the control of alcohol, they do not replace other measures, nor are they the most cost-effective means of reducing the level of societal alcohol-related problems. Yet, taking into consideration their feasibility and their necessity, particularly in combating the production and consumption of *aräqe* within the privacy of the home, we recommend the inclusion of the following measures in the national scheme for the control of *aräqe* in particular and alcohol and narcotics in general:

i. Awareness creation as regard the long-term consequence and impacts of *aräqe* (as well as other related alcoholic drinks and drugs) on individuals as well as the society through sustained campaigns focusing particularly on the younger generation in schools, centers of worship, the army, etc., in the same way as the anti-HIV and AIDS campaign was launched and conducted.

ii. Inclusion of lessons on alcoholic drinks and narcotics and their related problems in general, and those of *aräqe* and *č'at* in particular, in all high school syllabi.

iii. Inclusion of awareness raising programs on alcoholic drinks and narcotics and their related problems in general, and those of *aräqe* and *č'at* in particular, in the national health extension package.

iv. Encouragement of the formation of anti-alcohol clubs in schools and similar other institutions.

v. Prohibition of driving after drinking more than a specified amount of alcohol.

Though we recognize the wisdom of taking issue with all of these measures that seek to change individual behavior, we are inclined to believe that there is a second level of intervention that holds better promise of reducing alcohol-related problems much quicker.

8.2.2 Regulative Measures on the Environment Surrounding Individuals

For the above reasons, we consider the second category of action, namely, that which focuses on the environment surrounding individuals to constitute the main way forward so as to bring its harmful effects within acceptable limits. Regulating *the production and marketing of aräqe* in order to restrict its availability, improve its quality, control the places and the times of its sale, and bring it into the arena of legitimate business is possible, and cost-effective. Moreover, it is capable of addressing the long-term interest of all stakeholders: distillers, wholesalers, retailers, consumers, non-consumers, community-based and civil society organizations, development agents, as well as national-, regional-, and local-level state administrative organs and social service agencies.

Such institutional measures are not only doable but also just. There is no reason why the society should bear the brunt of providing for, caring for, and cleaning up the mess that is left behind by those that choose to drink beyond their limits. In other words, regulatory steps that reduce the social cost of *aräqe* either by restricting its availability or by internalizing the costs that remain as externalities through such devices as taxation are only fair.

Following in part the organizing principle of the *typology of alcohol controls* developed by Room and his colleagues (2002, 200-210), we present the outlines of the regulatory measures that we recommend on the basis of the findings of our study. These are classified by the *object of the regulation* under three major interrelated headings: (a) *regulation of the product itself,* (b) *regulation of the provider or seller,* and (c) *regulation of the conditions of sale or provision*[24].

---

[24] The typology includes a fourth object of regulation, namely, *the buyer or consumer.* We have, however, left this out considering the fact that we have made no recommendations for restricting customers in terms of behavior while or after drinking, as such a measure would be impractical under the prevailing situation in Ethiopia.

a) *Regulation of the Product Itself*

   i. Regulate in terms of purity, safety, strength or amount by developing standards, applying quality control, mandatory ingredient and content labeling, and certification by the national Authority.

   ii. Upgrading of product, production methods and implements through the provision of technical advice and access to credit.

   iii. Upgrading the production methods through research on appropriate and safe production techniques, fuels, fuel efficient stoves, etc.

   iv. Research on possible alternative use of *aräqe*, such as its utilization as fuel, which can help create an alternative market for the bulk of the *aräqe* that is produced in the country, and thus reduce the amount that is available for human consumption without necessarily denying *aräqe* distillers their established livelihood.

   v. Where applicable, protection of the intellectual property rights of innovators through patenting[25].

b) *Regulation of the Provider or Seller*

   i. Minimum age limits for all waiters and waitresses serving in public outlets, be they employees or family members.

   ii. Prohibition of sex workers from simultaneously engaging in solicitation and waitressing at all alcohol outlets, including those of *aräqe*.

---

[25] It is noteworthy that some *aräqe* producers have already made attempts at obtaining patent on their special *aräqe* distillation technique. One such entrepreneur is Ato Kassa Gämächu of Zwaï (see footnote 13), who has gained fame for his uniquely flavored varieties of *aräqe* and a kind of whisky which he distills using his own recipe and technique. His expressed wish is for support in terms of legal protection through issuance of patent, business advice, and access to credit in order to raise his distillery to an industrial level.

c) *Regulation of the Conditions of Sale or Provision*

    i. Introducing mandatory requirement of alcohol sale license for any eatery or drinking establishment, or place of entertainment that serves alcohol including informally prepared drinks such as aräqe and t'äj.

    ii. Restriction of *aräqe* and other alcoholic drink outlets from being located within certain distance from schools, sports venues and other places of cultural and religious activities, as well as major highways.

    iii. Prohibition of the selling of *aräqe* and other alcoholic drinks to customers under a minimum age.

    iv. Restriction of the hours of the day during which *aräqe* outlets are open to the public, particularly placing a limit on the earliest hour they can open.

    v. Prohibition of *aräqe* and other alcoholic drinks from being served in tea rooms, restaurants, pool houses, video show places and the like that are open to unaccompanied under-age customers.

    vi. Encouragement of the sale of food items at all *aräqe* outlets.

    vii. Price control through taxes and other means in order to make *aräqe* not so easily affordable and accessible.

    viii. Levying a toll on *aräqe* and other homebrewed alcoholic beverages such as commercial *t'äj* – in order to discourage the possible shift that would only move the problem somewhere else – at a level that is commensurate with the costs society incurs on account of the negative impacts of *aräqe* production, marketing, and consumption, and to be used expressly for the purpose of covering those costs.

8.2.3 *Working out and Enforcing the Regulation of Aräqe*

The setting up of a regulative arrangement that hopefully includes at least some of the above-listed measures is absolutely essential and of great urgency. Fortunately, the country finds itself at a most opportune moment in this regard. The important international and national legislative and institutional breakthrough of the last eight months that are discussed at length under Section

7.2 have come at the right time and opened new possibilities to deal with alcoholic drinks in general and those that are produced and marketed in the informal sector in particular in a comprehensive and systematic manner. It is therefore against the backdrop provided by this changing situation in the legislative and institutional environment that we recommend the following measures that relate to the working out and enforcement of the regulation of *aräqe*. Specifically, we recommend that FMHACA consider the following in the revision of its draft scheme for regulating the bulk production of all alcohol, including those at the cottage industry level:

i. Make the regulatory scheme comprehensive enough to address issues of *aräqe* and its related problems.

ii. Follow the guidelines provided by the Global Strategy to Reduce the Harmful Use of Alcohol, to which Ethiopia is a signatory.

iii. Critically examine and make use of research findings and recommendations, including those of this study.

iv. Strengthen, and upgrade the team within the FMHACA that is exclusively responsible for food to the level of a department or unit with tasks that include regulating marketed alcohol in general and alcohol produced in the informal sector such as *aräqe* in particular.

v. Implement, guide, and oversee the implementation of the regulatory scheme through its own branches as well as those of the regional and *wäräda* agencies or units, as per the provisions of Proclamation No. 661/2009, with particular emphasis and vigilance concerning *aräqe* and other alcoholic beverages produced in the informal sector for the market.

Obviously, the above are only sketches of what are needed. Their details and supplements need to be carefully worked out by FMHACA which is the sole executive Authority legally empowered to undertake the task. Hopefully, the Authority will join hands with other governmental and non-governmental actors, as well as other concerned stakeholders.

Annexes

Annex 1: Glossary of Local Terms

Absit: Small amount of malt flour that is boiled until it thickens and added as fermenting agent to any cereal dough or mash.

Amole: Salt bar mined in the Danakil Depression area and that once served as a currency throughout the Ethiopian Highlands.

Aräqe bet: A tavern specializing in the sale of *aräqe*.

Aräqe or Yä-abäša aräqe (Also known as **Katikala**): A pure grain, traditional home-distilled beverage that is made from an assortment of cereals such as wheat, sorghum and maize.

Aswäč'i: Person who owns a distilling establishment, and, therefore, manages and supervises the production process.

Atäla: Dregs from fermented and distilled beverages. In the case of *aräqe*, dregs left behind after the fermented mash is boiled and the alcohol separated.

Awč'i: Worker employed to carry out the tasks of *aräqe* distilling.

Bïqïl: Malt

Boč'e, Kolombia: Third-rate or lowest quality *aräqe* from Arsi Nägälle so-known at its place of origin and in Sululta markets where it is sold, respectively.

Č'at: (*Chata Adulis*) is a plant whose green leaf is consumed as a stimulant by a considerable number of people in the Horn of Africa, East Africa and South Arabia.

Č'elle: Beads. In relation to *aräqe*, the term denotes the ring of foam that forms on the inside of the bottle containing *aräqe*, thereby signifying good quality.

Däje sälam: The inner grounds of an Ethiopian Täwahïdo Orthodox church that are within its closure.

Däräqot: Maize which is soaked in water for three days, roasted, sun-dried and then milled.

Dïfdïf: The main mash of fermented and distilled alcoholic drinks; it is made by giving body to the starter mash *(t'ïnsïs)* by adding processed cereal flour.

Gan: Big clay jar used as container for water, *t'äj*, *t'älla*, and also for fermenting mash in the preparation of traditional alcoholic beverages including that of *aräqe*.

Gešo (**Shiny-leaf Buckthorn**): African shrub or small tree in the family *Rhamnaceae*. The plant is used for nutrition, medicine or religious purposes. In Ethiopia, where the plant is known as *gešo*, it is used in a manner similar to hops.

Gïbt'o: *(Lupinus albus)* commonly known as 'White Lupin', is a leguminous plant usually grown as hedge, for erosion control, nitrogen fixation, or sometimes for human consumption.

Gït'am, Qob, Mädfia, Diffito: Small clay 'head cap' component of the traditional still which is used to seal the clay jar and connect it to the bamboo pipe.

Ïdïr: Indigenous voluntary association established primarily to provide mutual aid during burial and mourning and sometimes also to address other community concerns.

Ïndod: *(Sarcoca dodecandra)* is a trailing shrub or climber native to Tropical Africa, Southern Africa, and Madagascar. It is used as detergent as well as a poison to stun fish.

Ïnjära bet: Outlet specializing in the sale of *ïnjära*.

Ïnjära: Thin, flat bread made from fermented, yeast-risen dough of a variety of cereals such as wheat, barley, sorghum and *teff*.

Ïnkïrdad: False wheat, cockle, or darnel (*Lolium temulentum*) that is sometimes mixed with other cereals in making *aräqe qit'a* with the objective of giving potency to the distilled product.

Ïnkuro: Stir-roasted, moistened cereal flour that is used to give body to the starter mash, *t'ïnsïs*.

Ïnsät: (*E. ventricosum*) commonly known as "false banana", is a root crop widely grown in south and southwestern parts of Ethiopia.

Ïnsïra: Clay jar that is smaller than *gan* and used for similar purposes. In *aräqe* distillation, it is used for boiling the fermented *aräqe* mash, and thus makes up part of the traditional *aräqe* still.

Ïqub: Traditional rotating saving and credit temporary association that lasts for the duration of a single round until all members benefit.

Ïrq: The act of concluding peace between conflicting parties after mediation by elders.

Jïge, Däbo: Labor reciprocity arrangement usually in harvesting.

Kïrïstïna: Baptism or baptism ceremony.

Kosso: (*Hagenia abyssinica*) also known as African redwood, brayera, or hagenia; it is a species of flowering plant native to the high-elevation afromontane regions of central and eastern Africa.

Mädäfdäf: The act of giving body to the starter mash *(t'ïnsïs)* by adding processed cereal flour in order to create the main mash of fermented and distilled alcoholic drinks.

Mahbär, Sänbäte: Traditional club-like association of about a dozen or so persons organized to meet, celebrate, and bond around a certain religious figure that is common among Ethiopian Tewahedo Orthodox Christians.

Mäläkia: 50 ml shot glass that is used as the standard glass for serving *aräqe*.

Margäja: The outer grounds of an Ethiopian Täwahïdo Orthodox church, those immediately outside a church's enclosure.

Mät'änsäs: The act of creating the starter mash by mixing usually *gešo* and malt with water, and sometimes only *gešo* with water.

Matot: Circular seat for the large clay jar (*gan*), made from *ïnsät* leaves or any soft bark.

Nïfro: Boiled whole grain that is consumed as snack.

Qïrare: Watered down *t'älla*. It is produced by adding water to the *t'älla* mash for a second run after *t'älla* has already been extracted from it in the course of the first run.

Qit'a, Dabbe, Qälet'o: Flat bread baked from different cereals; in the preparation of *aräqe*, these are added into the *aräqe* starter mash (*t'ïnsïs*) to make the main mash by giving it body (*dïfdïf*).

Šämbäqo, Ašända, Mässabia: Bamboo pipe around which a wet rope is coiled, and forms the joint of the traditional still through which the condensing alcohol vapor travels from the boiling clay pot to the collecting metal canteen.

Šärätä: Third-rate or lowest quality *aräqe* in Dämbäč'a.

T'äj: Traditional mead brewed from honey and *gešo*.

T'älla bet: Tavern specializing in the sale of *t'älla, koräfe,* or *borde*.

T'älla, Koräfe, Borde: Traditional fermented beverages of slightly different texture, consistency and test brewed from all types of cereals, save for *t'ef*.

Täzkar, Qurban, Yä arba dïgïs: Commemorative feasts offered in remembrance of the departed by their family and kin.

T'eff: (*Eragrostis teff*) is a cereal grain species of lovegrass native to the northern Ethiopian highlands, now grown throughout the country and a major food grain used to make *ïnjära*.

T'ïnsïs: Starter mash.

Wadiat, Däqq, Goras: Clay, wooden, or metal bowl. In *aräqe* production, it forms part of the traditional still and serves to contain the cold water into which the metal canteen, where the alcohol vapor further condenses and accumulates is immersed.

Wäräda: District. The middle-level state administrative unit (with an elected council) lying between those of the Region and the *Qäbäle*, and often placed under the Zone which fulfils coordination purposes.

Wät': Generic term to refer to a variety of traditional stew or sauce made from different ingredients and in different ways.

Yä bunna sïni: The small, handleless, china coffee-cup commonly used for drinking *aräqe* in peoples' homes where glassware is in short supply, and therefore serves a double purpose.

Yä däsdäs: A feast or an invitation for a round of drinks and/or food offered to celebrate a happy event, accomplishment, or closure.

Yä färänj aräqe: A factory distilled and bottled pure grain unflavored or flavored (usually with anise) alcoholic drink; the manufactured equivalent of *yä-abäša aräqe*.

Yä fint'ïr: Rounds of drinks offered on closing a successful business deal, usually at the expense of the party that collects cash.

Yä gïbt'o aräqe: Aräqe made of *gïbt'o* instead of the commonly used cereals, namely, wheat, maize, and sorghum.

Yä izin: Food and/or drinks brought to a house of mourning by kin, friends, neighbors, and particularly fellow *ïdïr* members.

Yä mïdïr ïmbuway: *(Cucumis ficifolius A. Rich.)* is a climber plant the fruit of which is inedible. In some circles it is known by the *gï'ïz* term *ïs'ä mäläkot* and its roots are considered to have medicinal qualities.

Annex 2: Alcohol Commodity Chains in Developing Nations

	Design (Recipe)	Raw materials	Manufacturing	Imports	Distribution	Marketing	Advertising
Traditional	Communally-derived	Locally-grown	Local	None	At point of production, by producer/producing community	Barter-based or ceremonial, to local communities	Word of mouth or attached to festival days, by producers and their communities
Traditional industrial	Imitation of communally-derived product, now in local, private or public hands	Locally-grown	Local	None	Local or national by private or governmental producers	Cash-based	Price and quality-oriented
Peripheral "cosmopolitan" (Neocolonial)	Originally from colonial power or trading partners, now in local private hands	Mostly grown local to point of production	Local, in core nations or in or near colonial metropolis	Mainly distilled spirits and wines	By colonial political or economic authorities, or their private assignees	Scrip or cash based, tied to labour centers; to workers in colonial enterprise	Price and quality oriented, by employers and/or colonial authorities
Globalized ("marketing driven")	From global or regional transnational producers	Local, supplemented by globally-sourced inputs	Local under control of global transnationals	Mainly distilled spirits and fine wines	Regional of global, by transnational producers, their subsidiaries and licensees	Cash-based, targeting entire population via own-premise promotions, sponsorships, endorsements, holiday promotion	Culturally embedded, "life style" oriented, by global advertising agencies or their affiliates

SOURCE: Jernigan 2000 (cited in Room *et al.* 2002).

Annex 3: Distribution of FGDs and In-depth Interviews Conducted, by Study Site and Type of Participants/Interviewees

Study Wärädas and Towns	Sululta Wäräda a. Giorfo b. Dubar	Bassona Wärana Wäräda and Däbrä Birhan Town a. Qäyit b. KA 02 of Däbrä Birhan	Dämbäč'a Wäräda a. Yäšaboč b. KA 02 of Dämbäč'a	Čäha Wäräda a. Yäteq b. KA 02 of Imdibir	Arsi Nägälle Ditto	Total
Specific Study Urban and Rural Qäbäles						
FGD with Distillers, Distiller-Sellers, Sellers	2	1	1	1	-	5
FGD with Community Leaders[1]	2	1	1	1	-	5
FGD with Development Workers[2]	1	1	1	1	-	4
Total FGDs	**5**	**3**	**3**	**3**	-	**14**
IDI[3] with Distillers-Sellers	6	7	4	1	1	19
IDI with Children of Distillers or Distiller-sellers	4	2	2	-	-	8
IDI with Husbands of Distillers	-	1	-	-	-	1
IDI with People that are engaged in Long-distance and/or Local wholesale	2	3	2	-	-	7
IDI with Elders	2	-	-	-	-	2
IDI with Brokers/Testers	1	-	-	-	2	3
IDI with Health Workers	1	1	1	1	-	5
IDI with Police	1	2	2	1	-	6
IDI with Wäräda and Qäbäle Administrators	3	2	1	1	1	8
Total IDIs	**20**	**18**	**12**	**4**	**4**	**59**

1. CBO Leaders, Spiritual Leaders, Teachers, Businessmen & Businesswomen.
2. Agriculture, Health, and Micro and Small Enterprise Extension Workers; Teachers and NGO Project Staff/ Beneficiary Committee Members.
3. IDI = In-depth Interview.

Annex 4: *Aräqe* Production and Fuel Wood Consumption in Arsi Nägälle

The table below presents the result of a week-long recording of fuel wood supply to Arsi Nägälle town. While the first column shows the various means of transportation/ unit of measurement of the fuel wood supplied to the four major fuel wood markets of the town (namely, Board, Tureta, Mobil, and Atena-Tera), the second column shows the mean amount of fuel wood supplied by each means of transportation in a week.

Means of Transportation/Unit of Measurement	Mean Amount Supplied
Donkey load	3475.87
Donkey-drawn cart	707.86
Horse load	70.14
Woman load	60.29
Man load	1
Vehicle (3.6 tons)	3.56
Meter cube (supplied by association of fuel wood suppliers	173

SOURCE: Summarized from Nejibe (2008, 38).

Note: According to Nejibe (2008, 39), about 96% of the fuel wood sold in the above markets is used of *aräqe* distillation.

Annex 5: Alcohol-attributable DALYs by Disease Category and World Bank Region, 2001 (thousands of DALYs)

Disease category	Europe and Central Asia	Latin America and the Caribbean	Sub-Saharan Africa	Middle East and North Africa	East Asia and the Pacific	South Asia	High-income countries	World
Chronic disease								
Maternal and prenatal conditions	12	7	39	1	2	29	6	105
Cancer	526	296	635	25	2,820	189	1,103	5,594
Neuropsychiatric	2,159	3,315	1,035	89	4,726	1,444	4,752	17,600
Vascular	2,639	926	556	40	1,751	1,199	-2,488	5,209
Other non-communicable diseases	1,175	739	504	27	997	306	1,153	5,126
Subtotal chronic disease	6,511	5,283	2,769	182	10,296	3,167	4,526	33,634
Injury								
Unintentional	4,127	1,984	2,308	135	3,613	2,222	1,753	15,619
Intentional	1,822	1,872	1,074	9	927	567	571	6,755
Subtotal injury	5,949	3,856	3,382	144	4,540	2,789	2,324	22,374
Total DALYs attributable to alcohol	12,460	9,139	6,151	326	14,836	5,956	6,850	56,008
Total DALYs from all diseases	116,502	104,287	344,754	65,570	346,225	408,655	149,161	1,535,871
Proportion of DALYs attributable to alcohol (percent)	10.7	8.8	1.8	0.5	4.3	1.5	4.6	3.6

SOURCE: http://www.dcp2.org/pubs/DCP/47/Table/47.2

Annex 6: Characteristics of Adult Alcohol Consumption in Different Regions of the World 2000 (Population Weighted Averages)

WHO Region	Beverage type mostly consumed	Total consmptin[1]	% unrecorded of total[2]	% heavy drinkers[3]	% drinkers among males	% drinkers among females	Consumption per drinker[4]	Average drinking pattern[5]
Africa D (e.g. Nigeria, Algeria)	Mainly other fermented beverages	4.9	53	5.3	47	27	13.3	2.5
Africa E (e.g. Ethiopia, South Africa)	Mainly other fermented beverages and beer	7.1	46	10.3	55	30	16.6	3.1
Americas A (Canada, Cuba, the United States)	> 50% of consumption is beer, about 25% spirits	9.3	11	11.2	73	58	14.3	2.0
Americas B (e.g. Brazil, Mexico)	Beer, followed by spirits	9.0	30	9.1	75	53	14.1	3.1
Americas D (e.g. Bolivia, Peru)	Spirits, followed by beer	5.1	34	2.7	74	60	7.6	3.1
Eastern Mediterranean B (e.g. the Islamic Republic of Iran, Saudi Arabia)	Spirits and beer, but scarce data	1.3	34	1.5	18	4	11.0	2.0
Eastern Mediterranean D (e.g. Afghanistan, Pakistan)	Spirits and beer, but scarce data	0.6	56	0.1	17	1	6.0	2.4
Europe A (e.g. Germany, France, the United Kingdom)	Wine and beer	12.9	10	15.7	90	81	15.1	1.3
Europe B (e.g. Bulgaria, Poland, Turkey)	Spirits	8.3	41	8.8	72	52	13.4	2.9

WHO Region	Beverage type mostly consumed	Total consmptin[1]	% unrecorded of total[2]	% heavy drinkers[3]	% drinkers among males	% drinkers among females	Consumption per drinker[4]	Average drinking pattern[5]
Europe C (e.g. the Russian Federation, Ukraine)	Spirits	13.9	38	18.6	89	81	16.5	3.6
South-East Asia B (e.g. Indonesia, Thailand)	Spirits	3.1	27	1.2	35	9	13.7	2.5
South-East Asia D (e.g. Bangladesh, India)	Spirits	2.0	79	0.9	26	4	12.9	3.0
Western Pacific A (e.g. Australia, Japan)	Beer and spirits	8.5	20	4.2	87	77	10.4	1.2
Western Pacific B (e.g. China, the Philippines, Viet Nam)	Spirits	5.0	26	4.1	84	30	8.8	2.2

SOURCE: WHO (2004, 53)

[1] *Estimated total alcohol consumption per resident aged 15 and older in liters of absolute alcohol (recorded).*
[2] *Percentage of total adult per capita consumption (= column 3) which is estimated to be unrecorded.*
[3] *Estimated % rate of heavy drinking (males ≥ 40 g and females ≥ 20 g) among those aged 15+*
[4] *Estimated total alcohol consumption (in liters of absolute alcohol) per adult drinker.*
[5] *Estimated average pattern of drinking (1-4 with 4 being the most detrimental pattern i.e. based on many heavy drinking occasions, drinking outside meals, high level of fiesta drinking and drinking in public places, etc. and 1 being the least detrimental pattern i.e. least heavy drinking occasions, drinking with meals, no fiesta drinking, least drinking in public places, etc.)*

Annex 7: Symbols Used for the Transliteration of Ethiopian Words

Vowel	Symbol	Example	
1st order	ä	ዘፈነ	Zäffänä
2nd order	u	ሁሉ	hullu
3rd order	i	ሂድ	hid
4th order	a	ራራ	rarra
5th order	e	ቤት	bet
6th order	ï	እግር	ïgïr
7th order	o	ሆድ	hod

Consonant	Symbol	Example	
ሽ	š	ሸሸ	šäššä
ቀ	q	ቆቅ	qoq
ች	č	ቸረቸረ	čäräččärä
ኝ	ñ	ኞኞ	ñoñño
ዠ	ž	ዠር	gäž
የ	y	ይታይ	yïttay
ጀ	j	ጀግና	jägna
ጠ	t'	ጠጣ	t'ät'a
ጨ	č'	ተንጫጫ	tänč'ač'č'a
ጸ	p'	ጳውሎስ	P'awlos
ፀ	s'	ፀሐት	s'äs'ät
ሟ	mʷa	ለሟ	lmʷa

SOURCE: *Journal of Ethiopian Studies* (JES).

References

Abebaw Fekadu, Atalay Alem, and Charlotte Hanlon. 2007. Alcohol and drug abuse in Ethiopia: Past, present and future. *African Journal of Drug and Alcohol Studies* 6 (1): 39-53.

Abbink, Jon. 2005. Drinks. In *Encyclopaedia Aethiopica*, edited by S. Uhlig, 198 - 200. Vol. 2. Wiesbaden: Harrassowitz Verlag.

_____. 1997. Competing practices of drinking and power: Alcoholic "Hegemonism" in Southern Ethiopia. *Northeast African Studies* 4, No. 3 (New Series): 7-22

Adelekan, Moruf. 2008. Noncommercial alcohol in Sub-Saharan Africa. In *Noncommercial alcohol in three regions. ICAP Review* 3: 3-14. Blackburn, United Kingdom: International Center for Alcohol Policies.

Amoateng, Yaw Acheampong, Ishmael Kalule-Sabiti, and Prakash Narayanan. 2007. Substance use and sexual behaviour among African adolescents in the North-West Province of South Africa. *African Journal of Drug and Alcohol Studies* 6 (1): 27-38.

Andargatchew Tesfaye. 1988. *The crime problem and its correction*. Vol. I. Department of Sociology and Social Administration. Addis Ababa University.

Bennett, L. A., C. Campillo, C. Chandrashekar, and O. Gureje. 1998. Alcoholic beverage consumption in India, Mexico and Nigeria. *Alcohol health and research world* 22 (4): 243-252.

Blue, Anthony Dias. 2004. *The complete book of spirits: A guide to their history, production, and enjoyment*. New York: HarperCollins.

Diamond, Jared. 1997. *Guns, germs, and steel: A short history of everybody for the last 13,000 years*. London: Vintage.

Endalew Addis. 2008. The socioeconomic impacts of Katikala production and consumption in Arsi-Negelle *Wäräda* of Oromia Region, Ethiopia. MA Thesis, College of Development Studies, Addis Ababa University. (Unpublished).

Ezzati, M. and D. Kammen. 2002. The health impacts of exposure to indoor air pollution from solid fuels in developing countries: Knowledge, gaps, and data needs - Resources for the future. Discussion Paper 02-24. Washington, D.C.

Federal Democratic Republic of Ethiopia Population Census Commission. 2008. *Summary and Statistical Report of the 2007 Population and Housing Census.* Addis Ababa.

Federal Democratic Republic of Ethiopia. 2010. Federal Negarit Gazeta, 16th Year, No. 9, 29th June 1999. Addis Ababa.

_____. 1999. Federal Negarit Gazeta, 5th Year, No. 60, 29th June 1999. Addis Ababa.

Gaur, Kadambini. 2006. *Process optimization for the production of ethanol via fermentation.* Patiala, India: Thapar Institute of Engineering and Technology, Deemed University.

Hannigan, John. 2006. *Environmental Sociology.* New York: Routledge.

http://chestofbooks.com/flora-plants/weeds/Poisonous-Plants/Grass-Family-Gramineae-Darnel-Lolium-temulentum-L.html

http://www.pfaf.org/database/plants.php?Lupinus+albus+graecus

http://www.eol.org/pages/703662

http://www.henriettesherbal.com/eclectic/usdisp/lupinus.html

Kelleher K. J., and J. M. Robbins. 1997. Social and economic consequences of rural alcohol use. *NIDA Research Monograph*, No. 168: 196-219.

Klingemann, H. 2001. *Alcohol and its social consequences – The forgotten dimension.* Dordrecht: Kluwer Academic Publishers.

Liyanage, U. 2008. Noncommercial alcohol in Southern Asia: The case of Kasippu in Sri Lanka. *ICAP Review* 3:24-34.

Mesaki, S. 1995. Alcoholisation in Third World countries. *UTAFITI* (New Series) 2 (1 & 2): 132-142.

Davis, W. Thomas. 2006. Distillation. *Microsoft Encarta.* Microsoft Corporation.

Microsoft Encarta. 2006. "Psychotropic drugs." Microsoft Corporation.

Microsoft Encarta [DVD]. 2009. "Rum Rebellion." Microsoft Corporation.

Morris, C. N., B. Levine, G. Goodridge, N. Luo, and J. Ashley. 2006. Three-country assessment of Alcohol-HIV related policy and programmematic responses in Africa. *African Journal of Drug & Alcohol Studies* 5 (2): 170-184.

Nejibe Mohammed. 2008. Impact of Katikala production on the degradation of woodland vegetation and emission of CO and PM during distillation in Arsi-Negelle *Wäräda*, Central Rift Valley of Ethiopia. MSc Thesis. Addis Ababa University.

Pankhurst, Richard. 1990. *A social history of Ethiopia: The northern and central highlands from early Medieval times to the rise of Emperor Tewodros II*. Addis Ababa: Institute of Ethiopian Studies, Addis Ababa University.

Pankhurst, Richard. 1965. *Travellers in Ethiopia*. London: Oxford University Press.

Parliament of Victoria Drugs and Crime Prevention Committee. 2004. Inquiry into Strategies to Reduce Harmful Alcohol Consumption. Discussion Paper.

Reader, John. 1998. *Africa: A biography of the continent*. London: Penguin Books.

Room, Robin, David Jernigan, Beatriz Carlini-Marlatt, Oye Gureje, Klaus Mäkelä, Mac Marshall, Maria Elena Medina-Mora, Maristela Montreiro, Chalrles Parry, Juha Partanen, Leane Riley, and Shekhar Saxena.2002. *Alcohol in developing societies: A public health approach*. Vol. 46. Helsinki: Finnish Foundation for Alcohol Studies, in collaboration with World Health Organization.

Social Issues Research Centre (SIRC). 1998. *Social and cultural aspects of drinking*. Oxford, UK: SIRC.

Transitional Government of Ethiopia. 1993a. *The national drug policy of the Transitional Government of Ethiopia*. Addis Ababa.

_____. 1993b. *The health policy of the Transitional Government of Ethiopia*. Addis Ababa.

UNDP. 1995. The social impact of drug abuse. No. 2.

United Nations. 1961. Single Convention on Narcotic Drugs.

_____. 1971. Convention on Psychotropic Substances.

_____. 1988. Convention against the Illicit Traffic in Narcotic Drugs and Psychotropic Substances.

World Health Organization (WHO). 2000. *International guide for monitoring alcohol consumption and related harm*. Department of Mental Health and Substance Dependence, Noncommunicable Diseases and Mental Health Cluster, World Health Organization.

_____. 2004. *WHO Global Status Report on Alcohol*. Geneva: WHO.

_____. 2007. *Second Report of the WHO Expert Committee on Problems Related to Alcohol Consumption*. WHO Technical Report Series, no. 944. Geneva: WHO.

_____. 2010. Strategies to reduce the harmful use of alcohol: Draft global strategy. Report by the Secretariat. Sixty-Third World Health Assembly. Provisional agenda item 11.10. A63/13.

Wirth, Louis. 1938. Urbanism as a way of life. *American Journal of Sociology* 44: 1-24.

Wolde T. 1999. Employment and income in the urban informal sector: A case study of Katikala Producers in Assala town. MA Thesis, Addis Ababa University.

አለቃ ተክለ ኢየሱስ. 2002. *የኢትዮጵያ ታሪክ: ሐተታ በስርጉው ገላው:: ብርሃንና ሰላም ማተሚያ ድርጅት:: አዲስ አበባ::*

CPSIA information can be obtained at www.ICGtesting.com
Printed in the USA
LVOW12s0959211113

362233LV00002B/414/P